Dream a little Dream

A Day

Cindy Norris

Published in 2016 through

Create Space

Available on Amazon.com and from the author/illustrator.

For more information, contact the author/illustrator at
cindyjnorris@gmail.com.

ISBN 978-1530372317

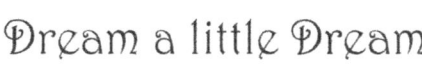

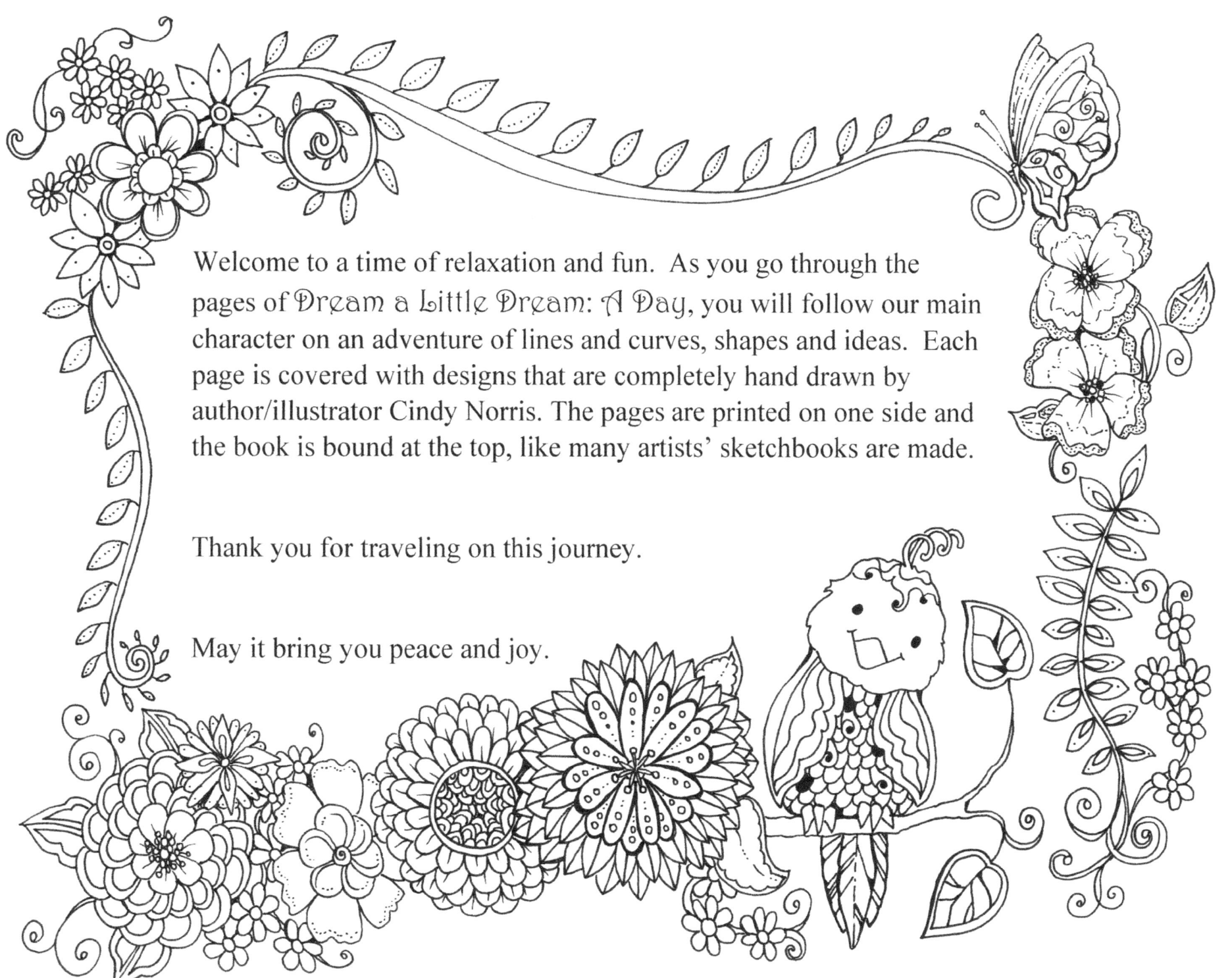

Welcome to a time of relaxation and fun. As you go through the pages of Dream a Little Dream: A Day, you will follow our main character on an adventure of lines and curves, shapes and ideas. Each page is covered with designs that are completely hand drawn by author/illustrator Cindy Norris. The pages are printed on one side and the book is bound at the top, like many artists' sketchbooks are made.

Thank you for traveling on this journey.

May it bring you peace and joy.

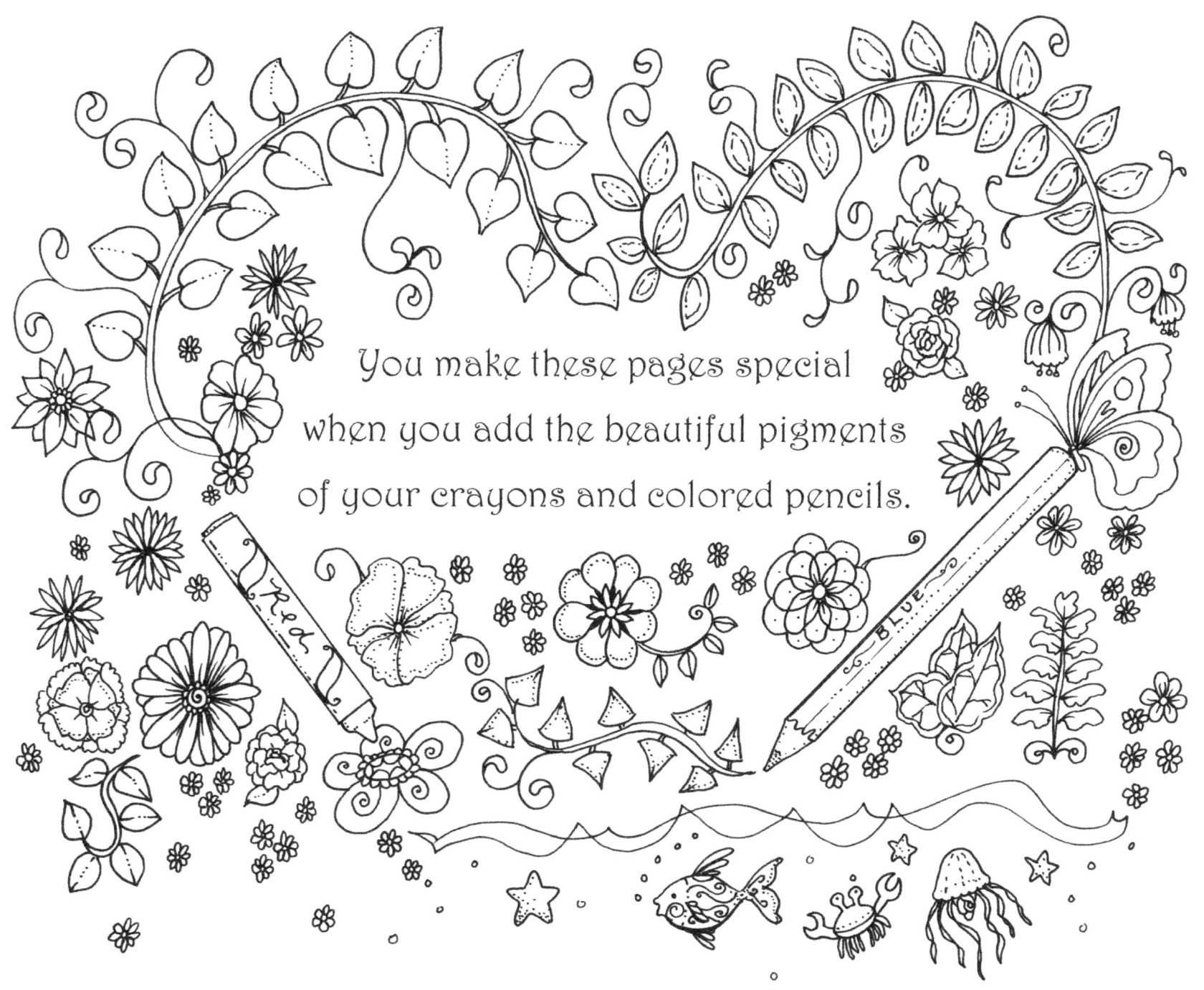

You make these pages special
when you add the beautiful pigments
of your crayons and colored pencils.

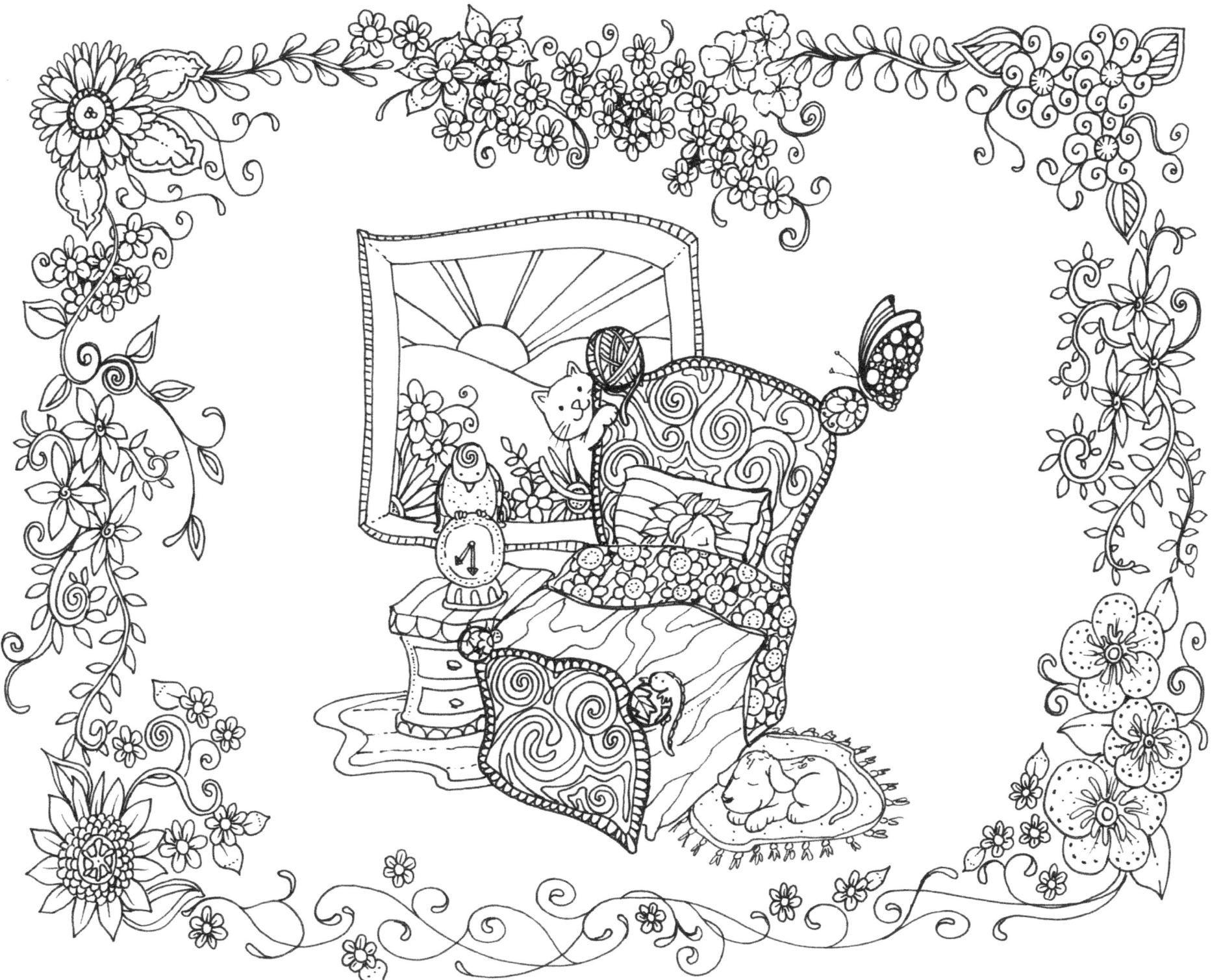

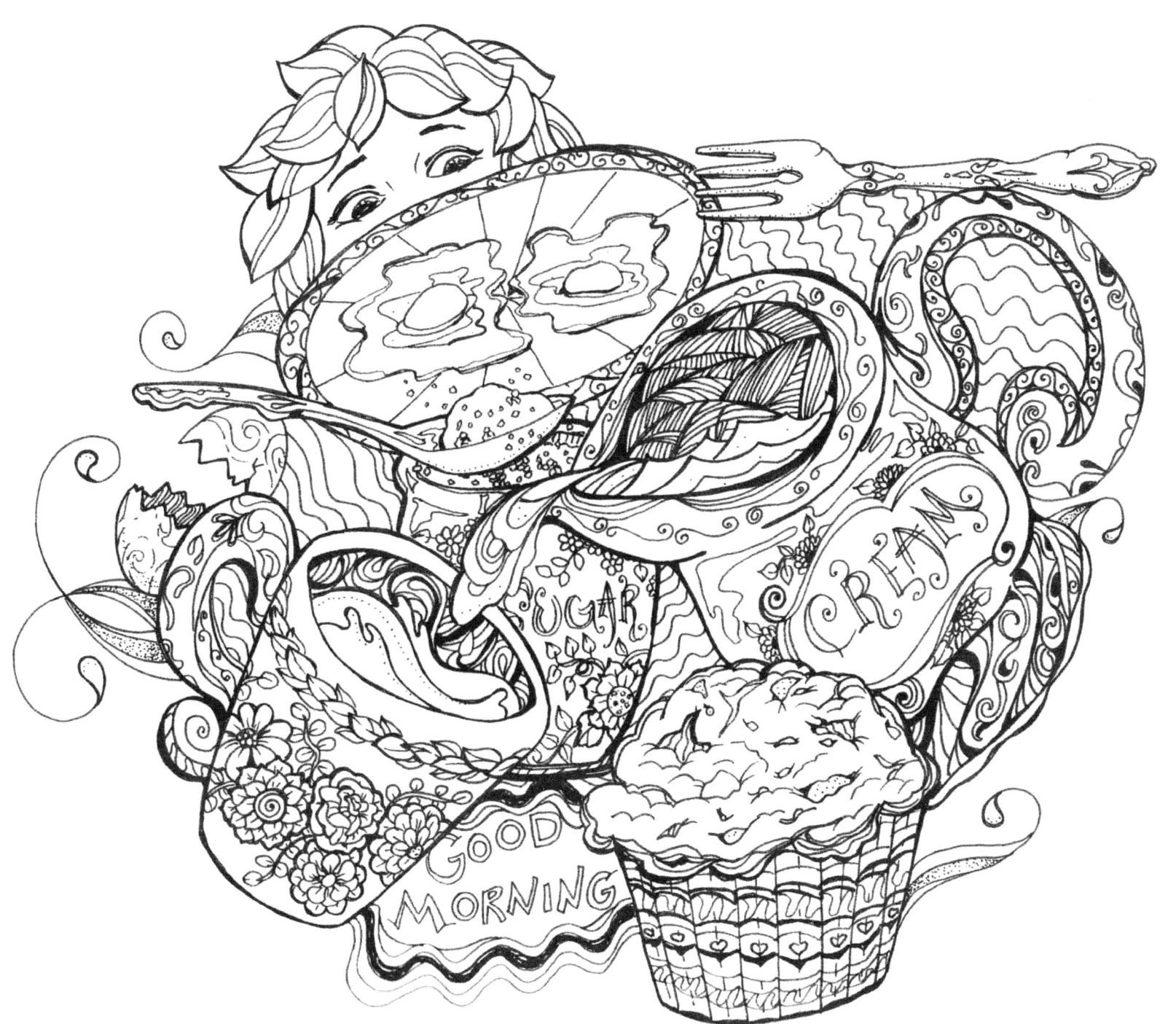

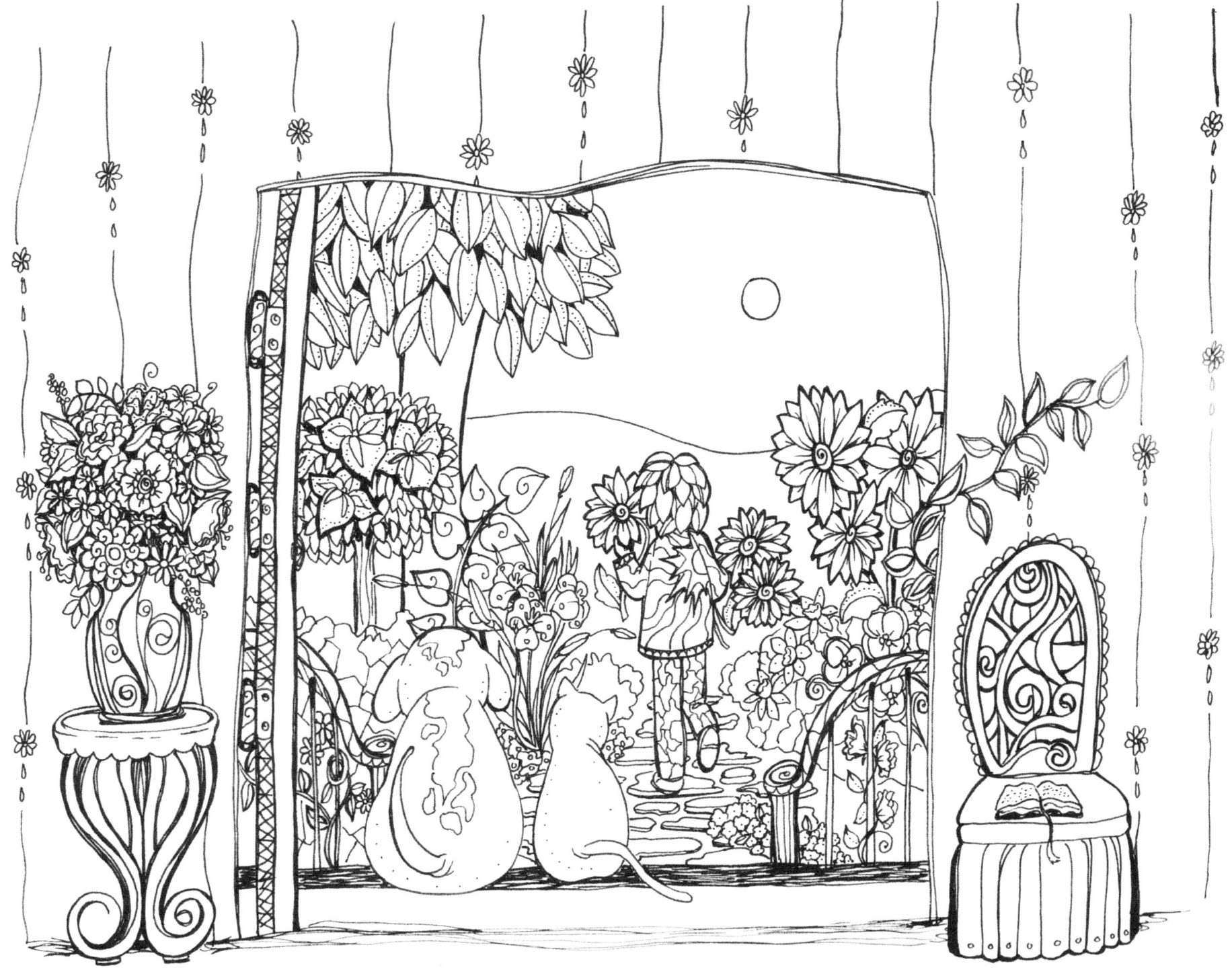

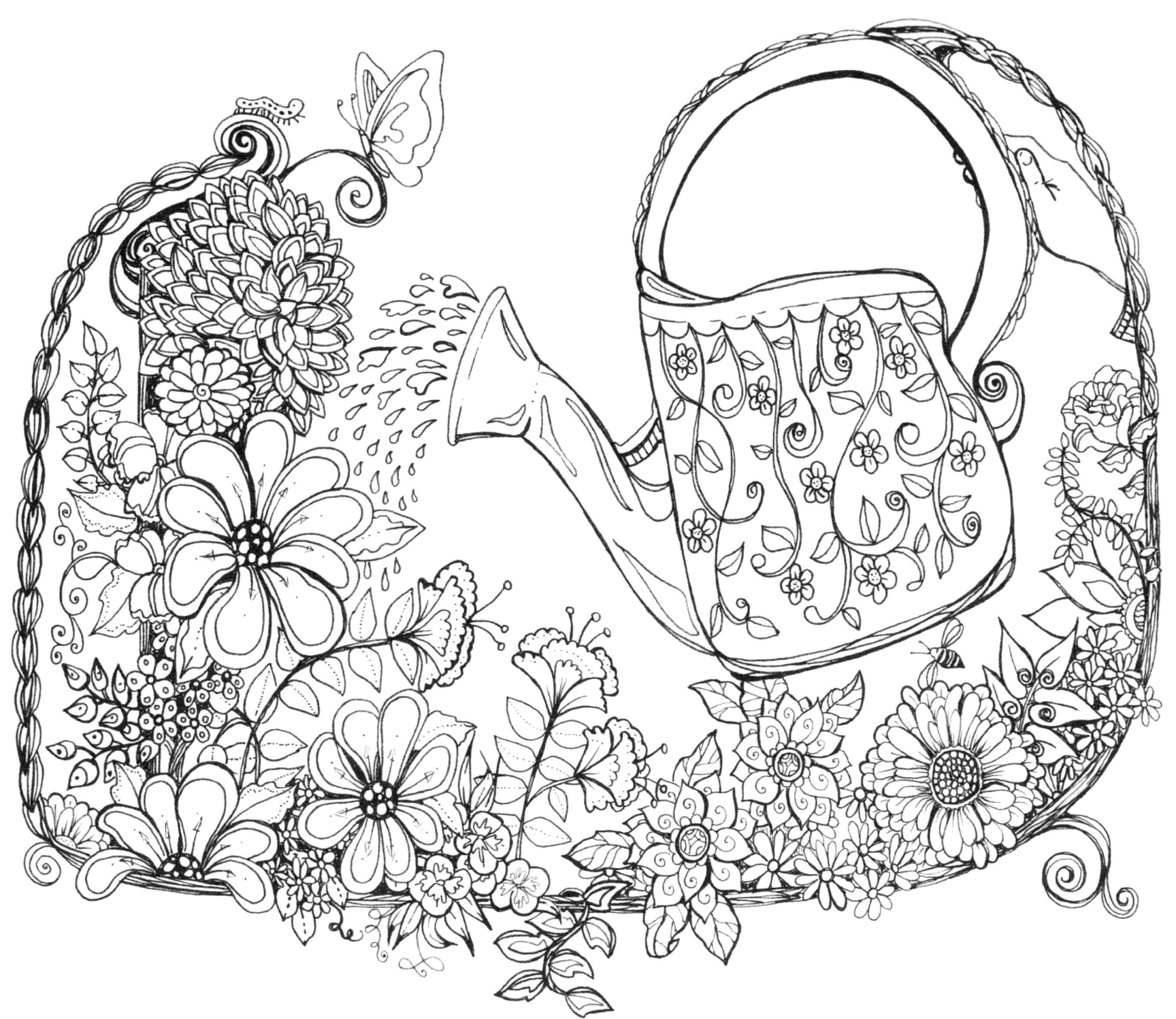

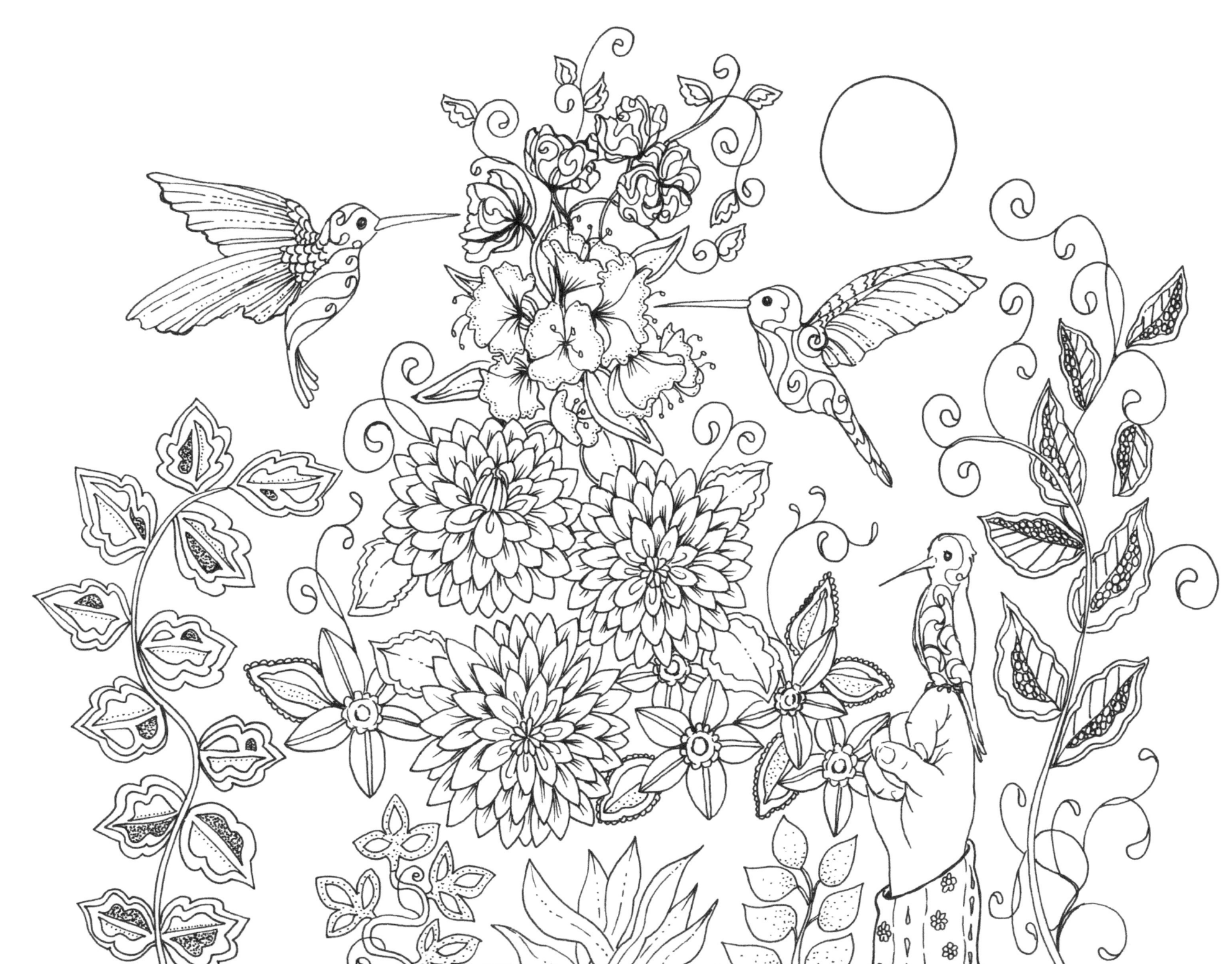

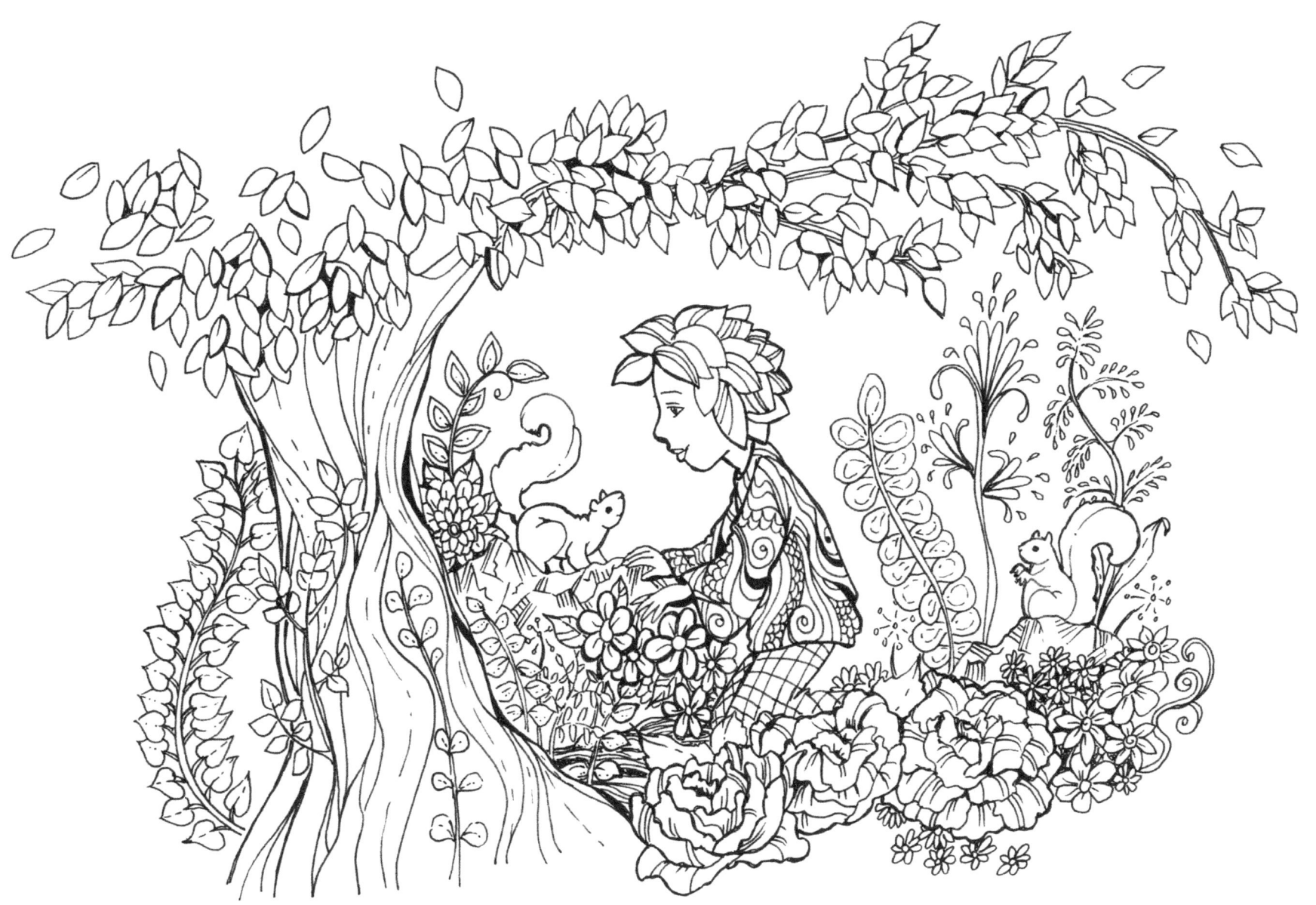

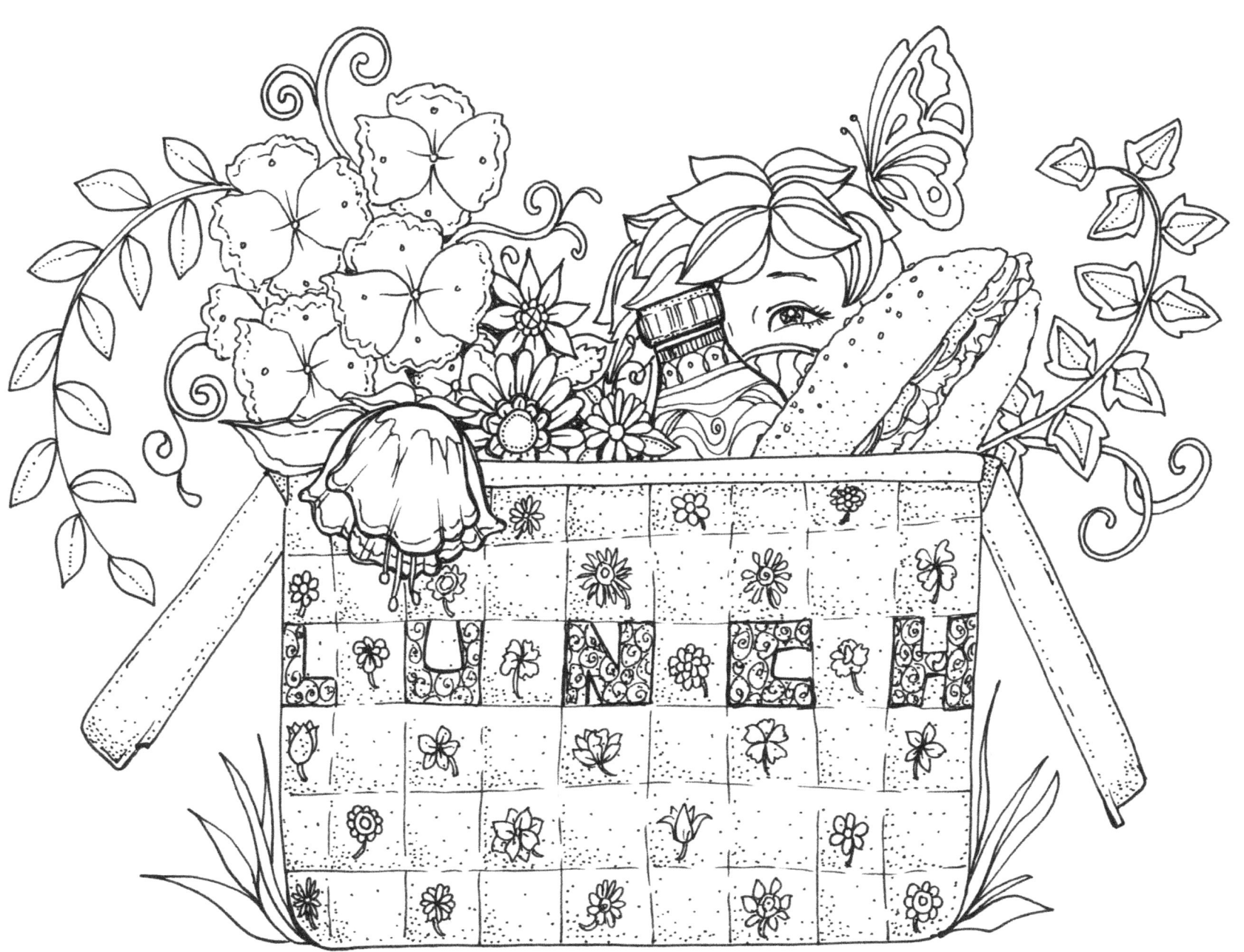

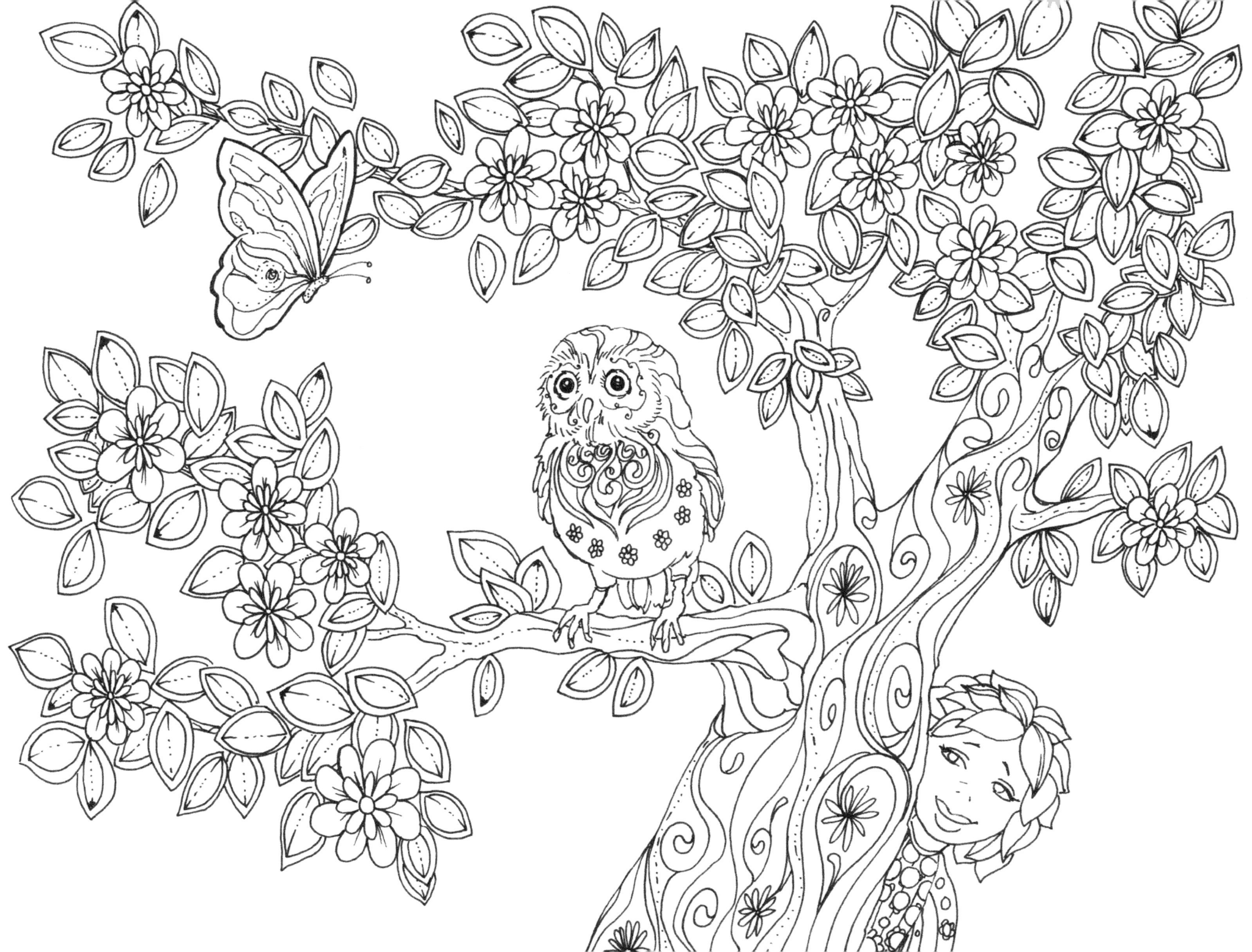

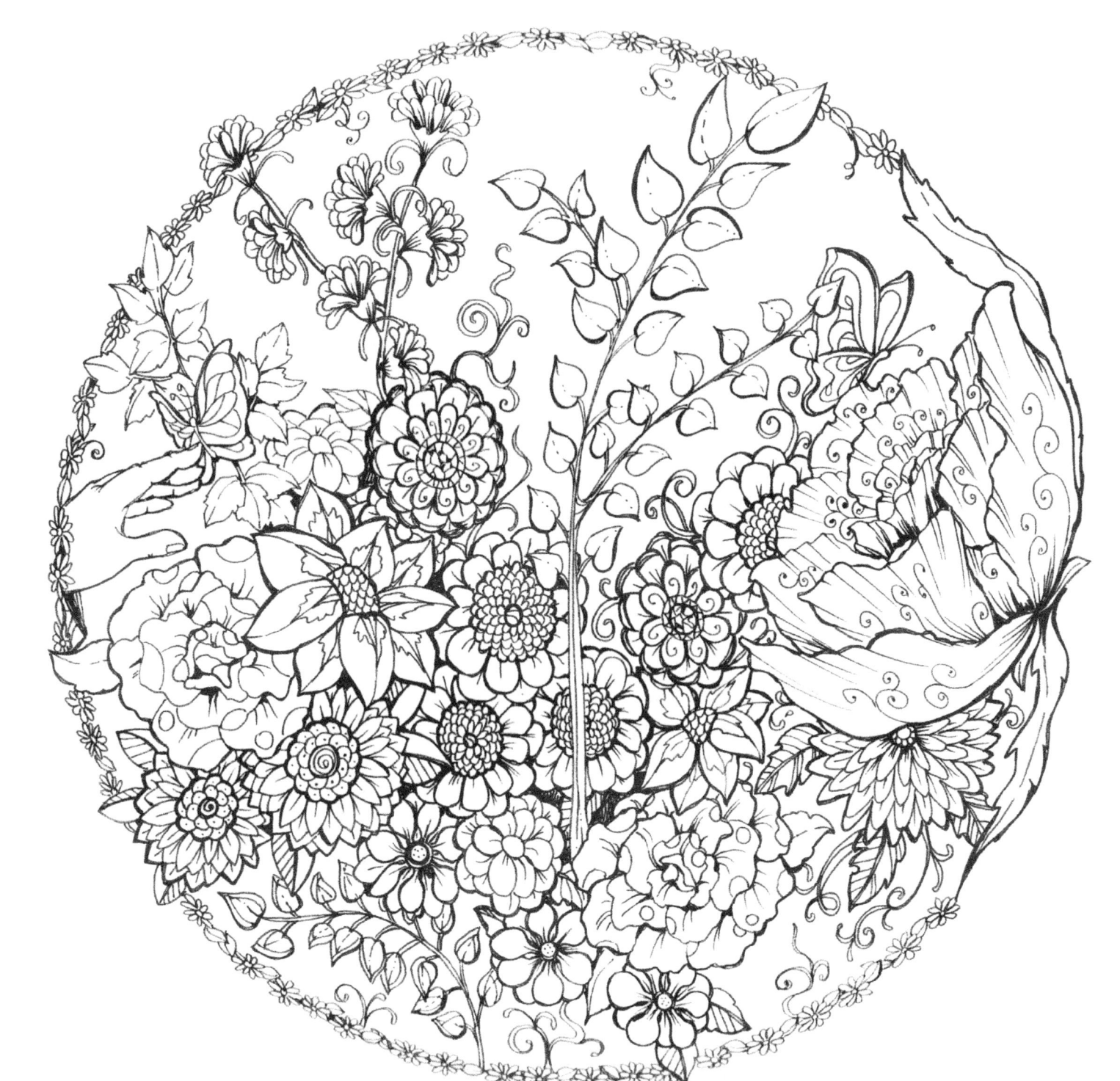

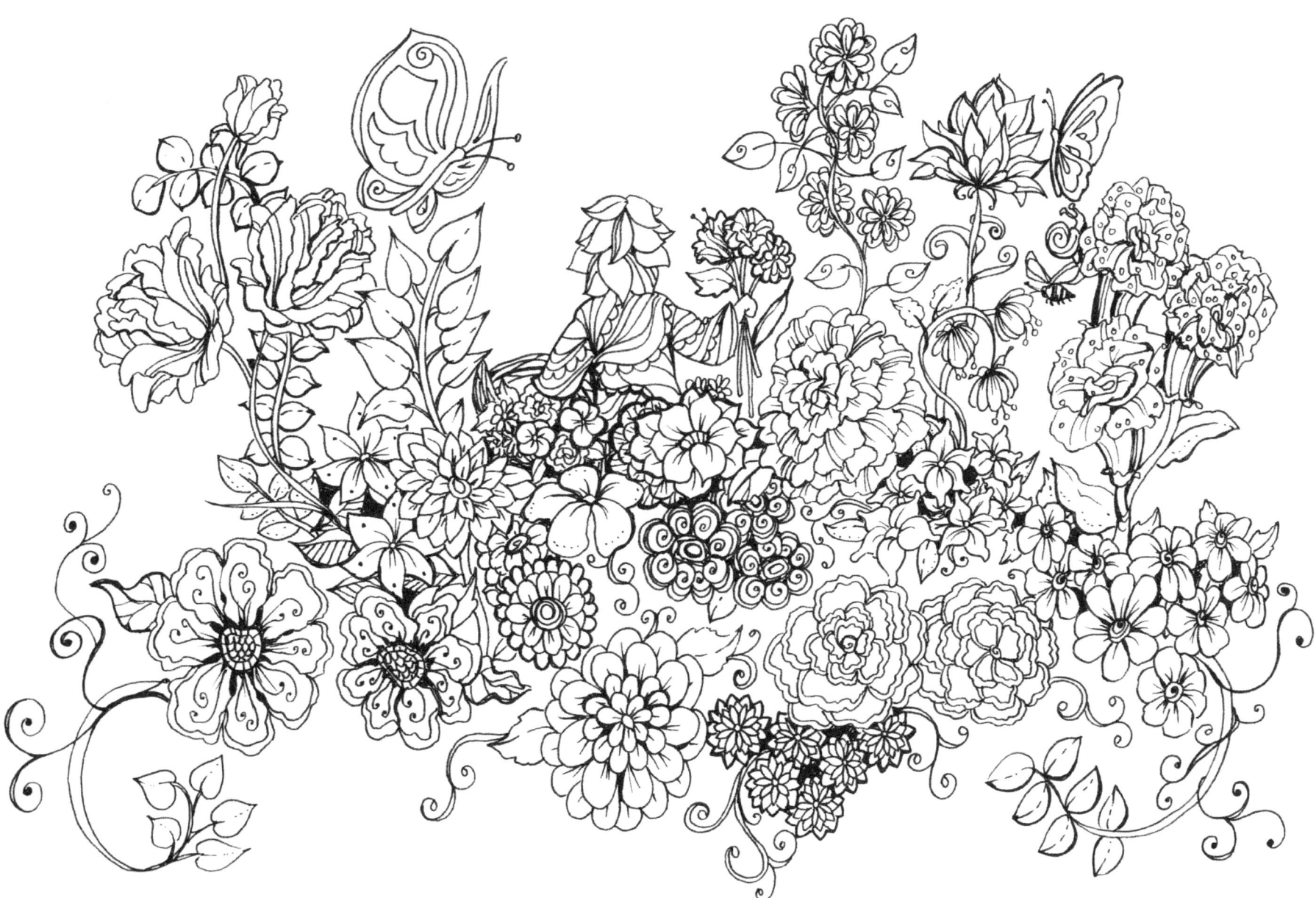

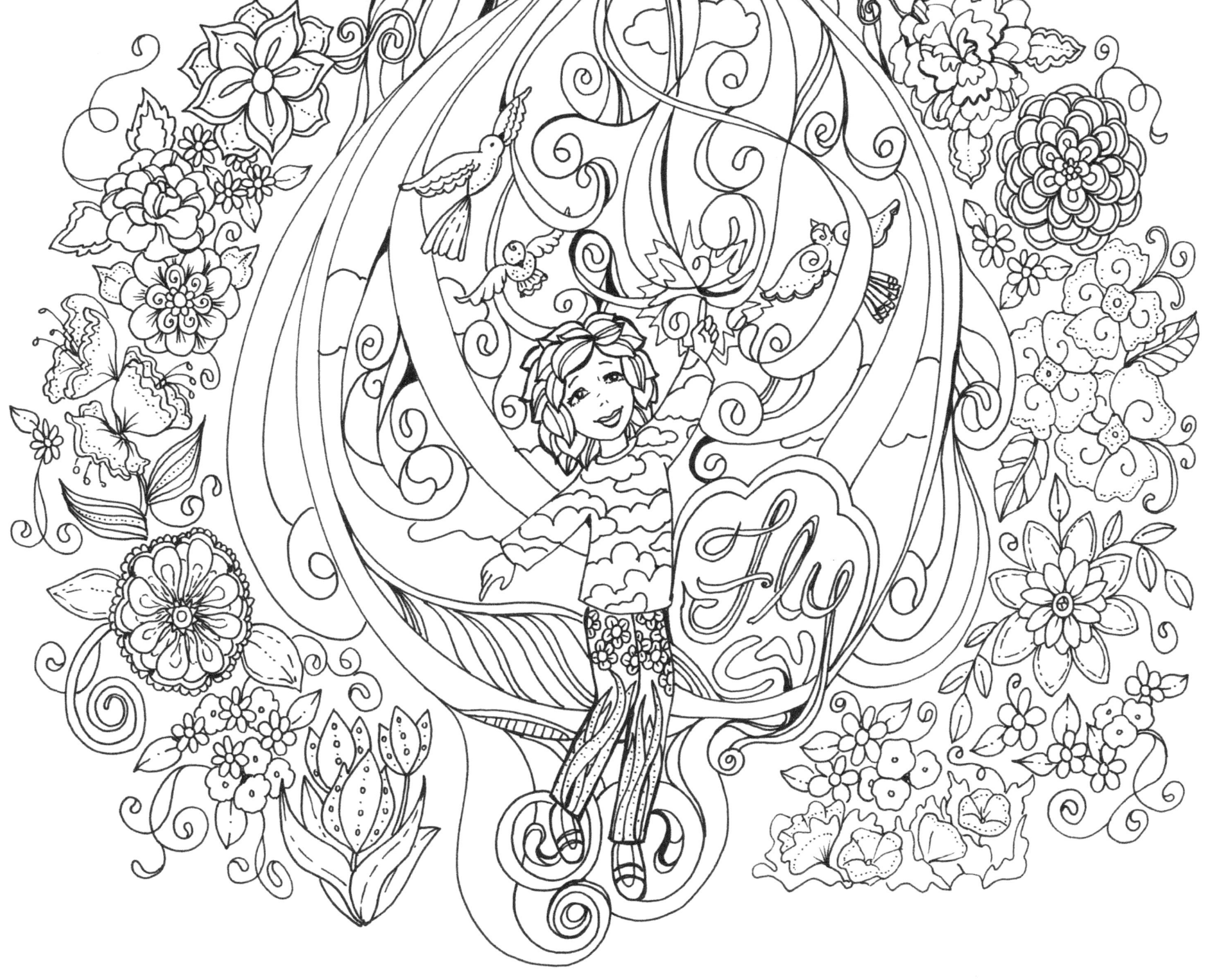

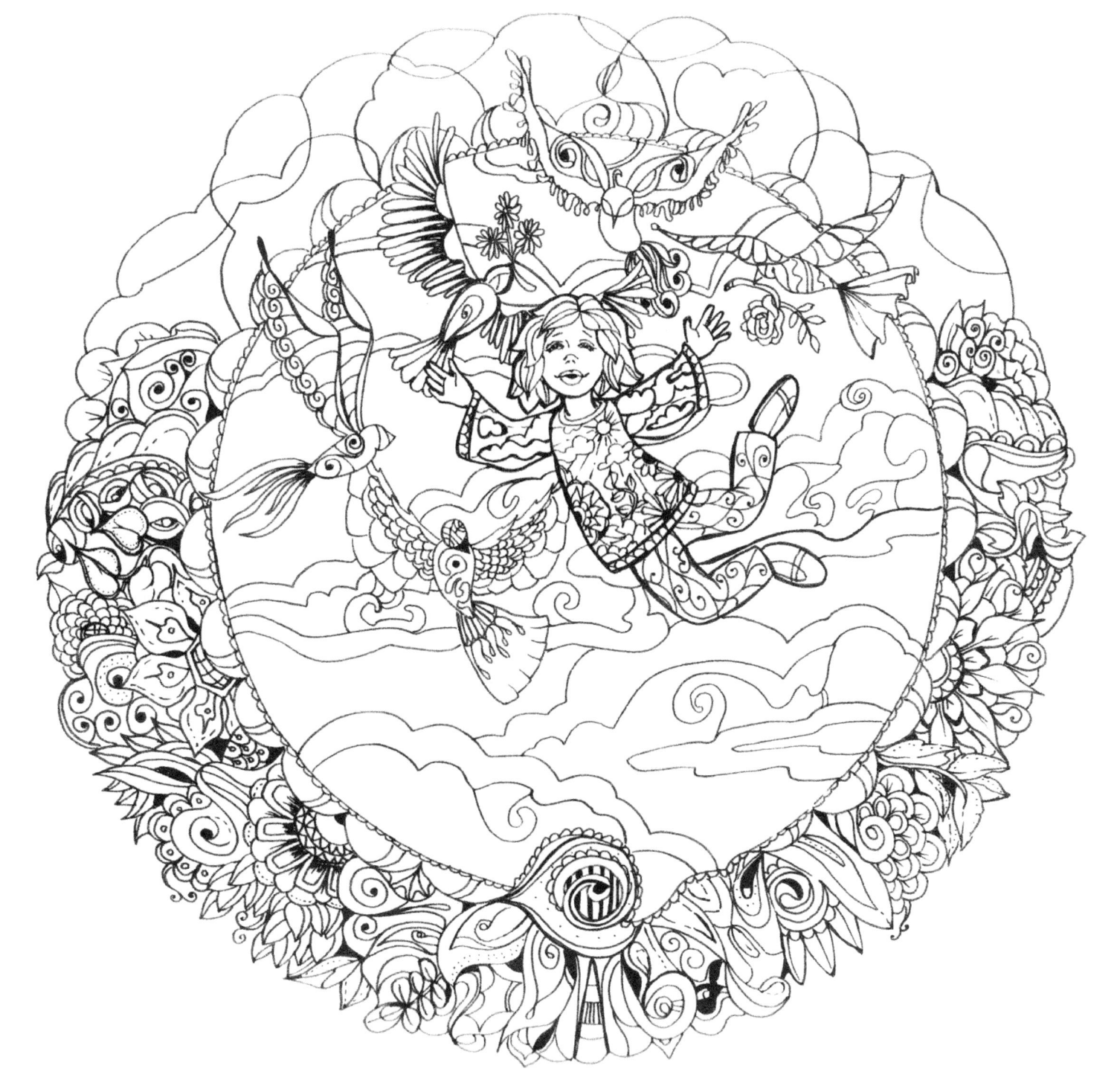

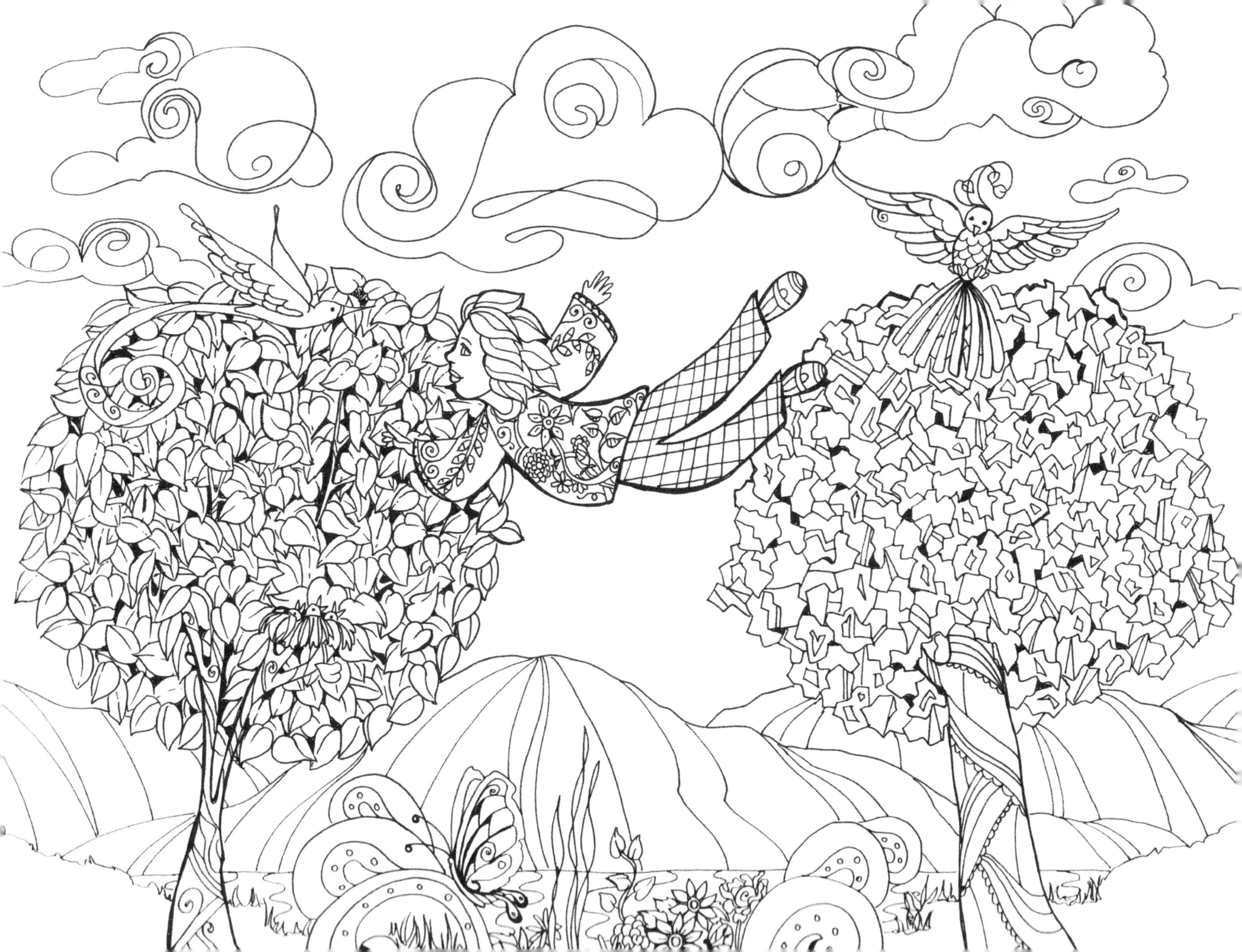

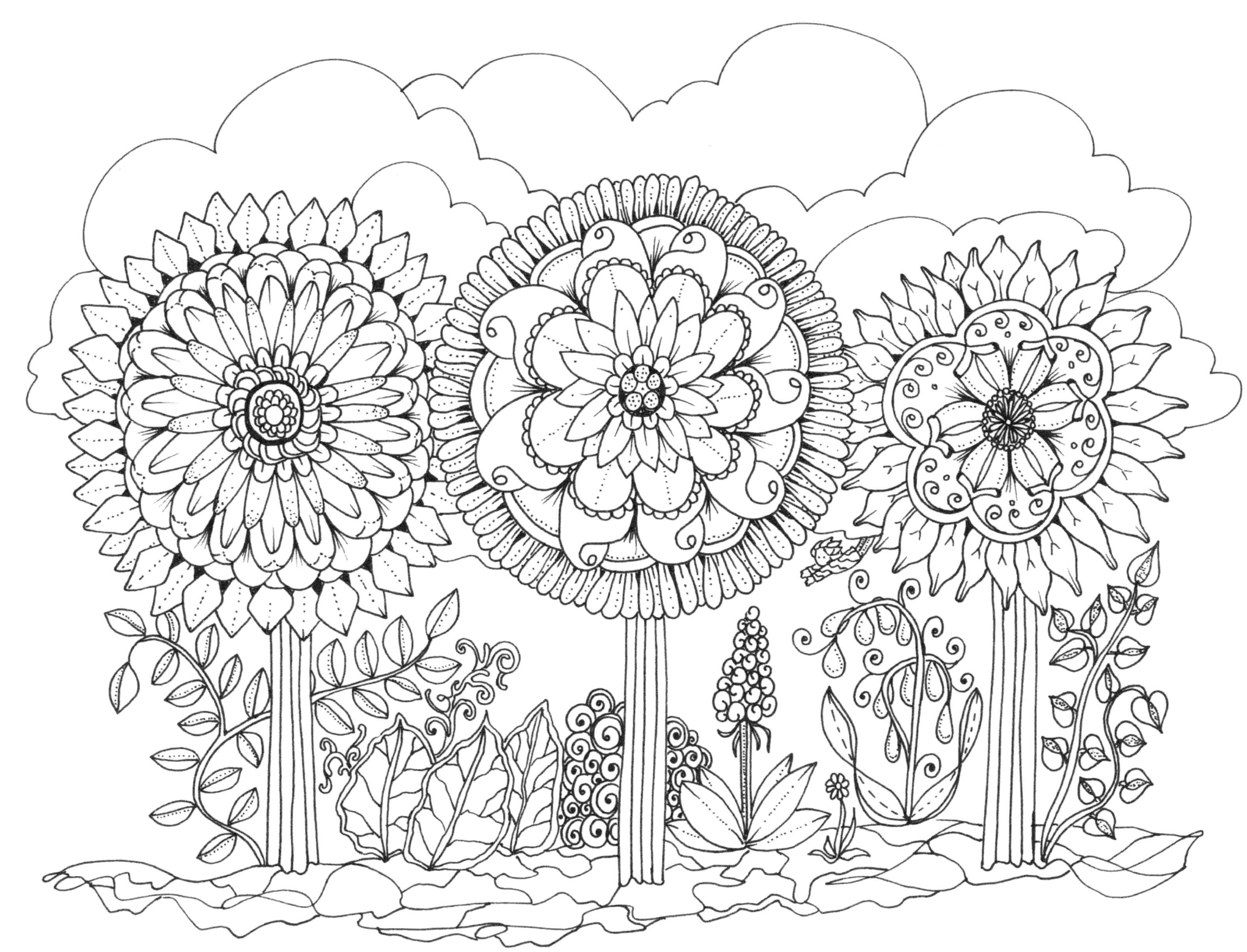

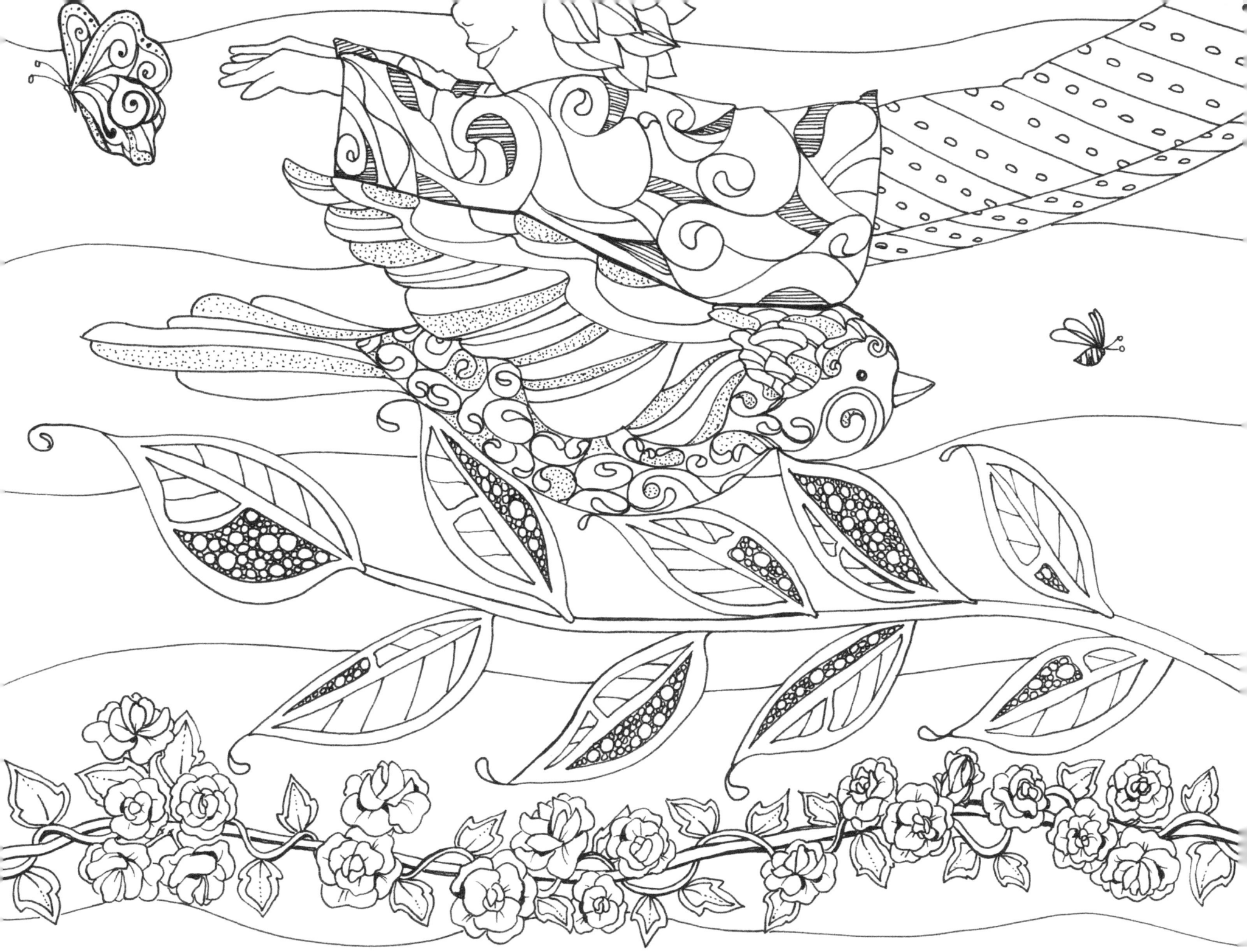

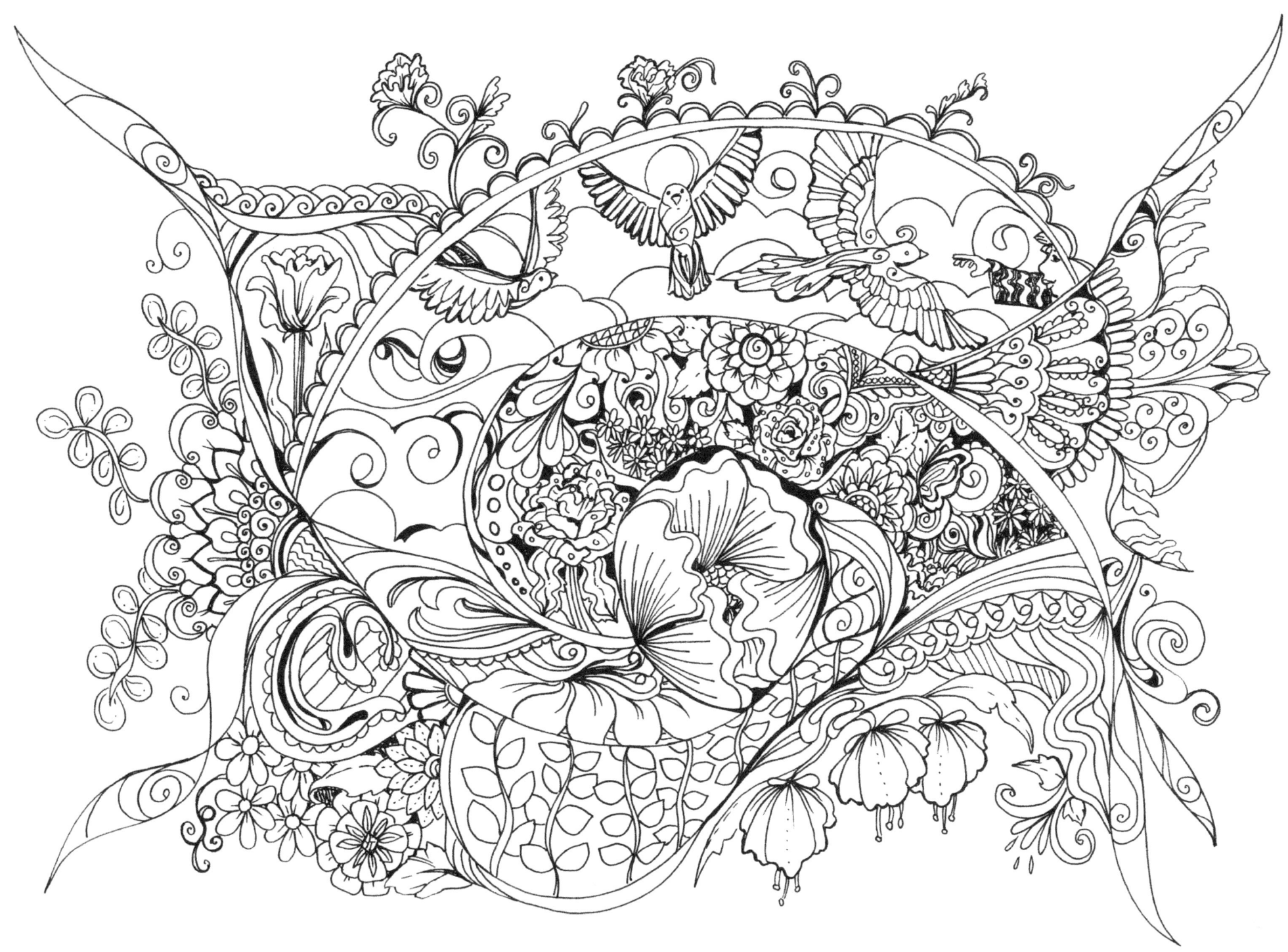

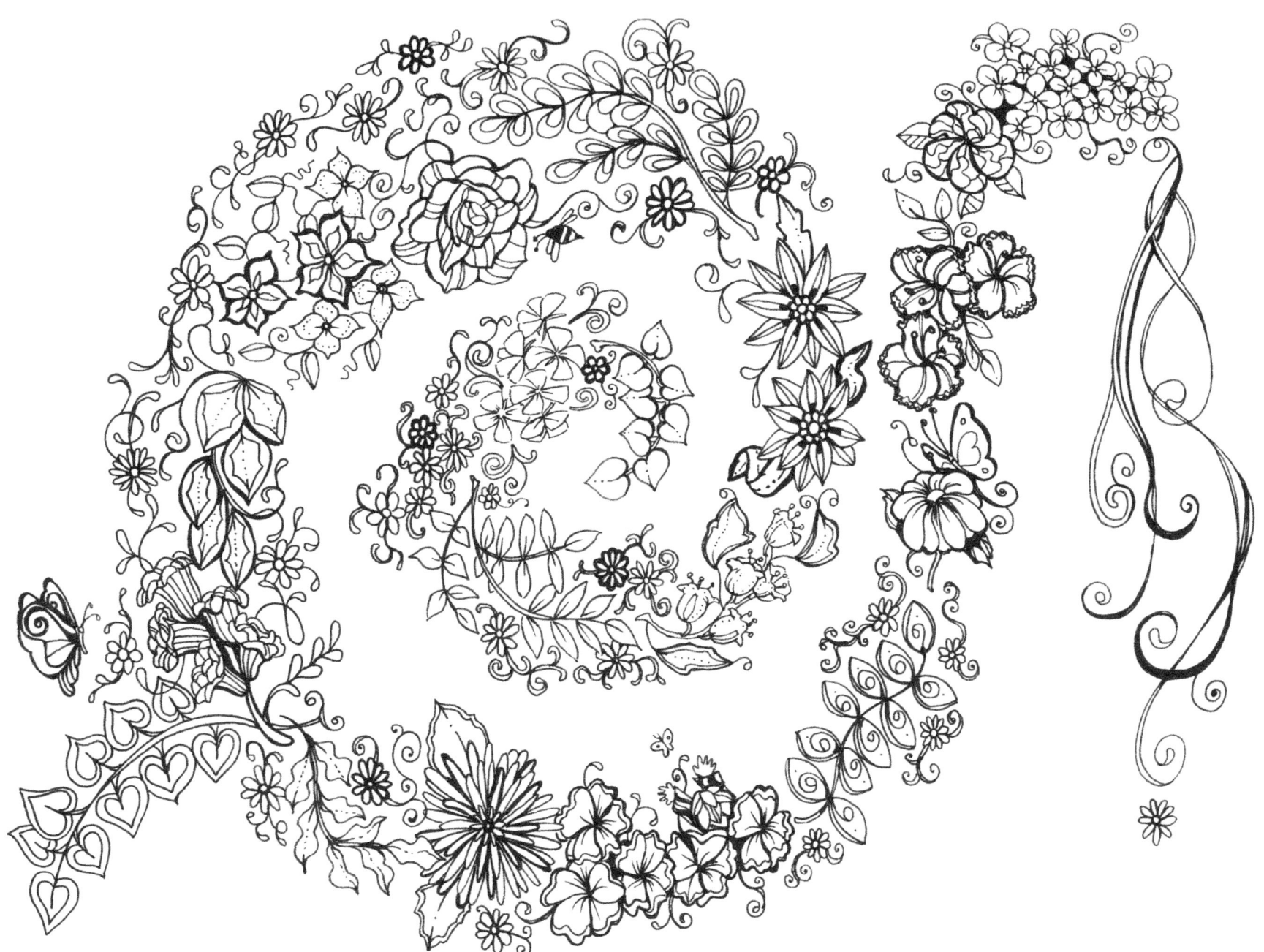

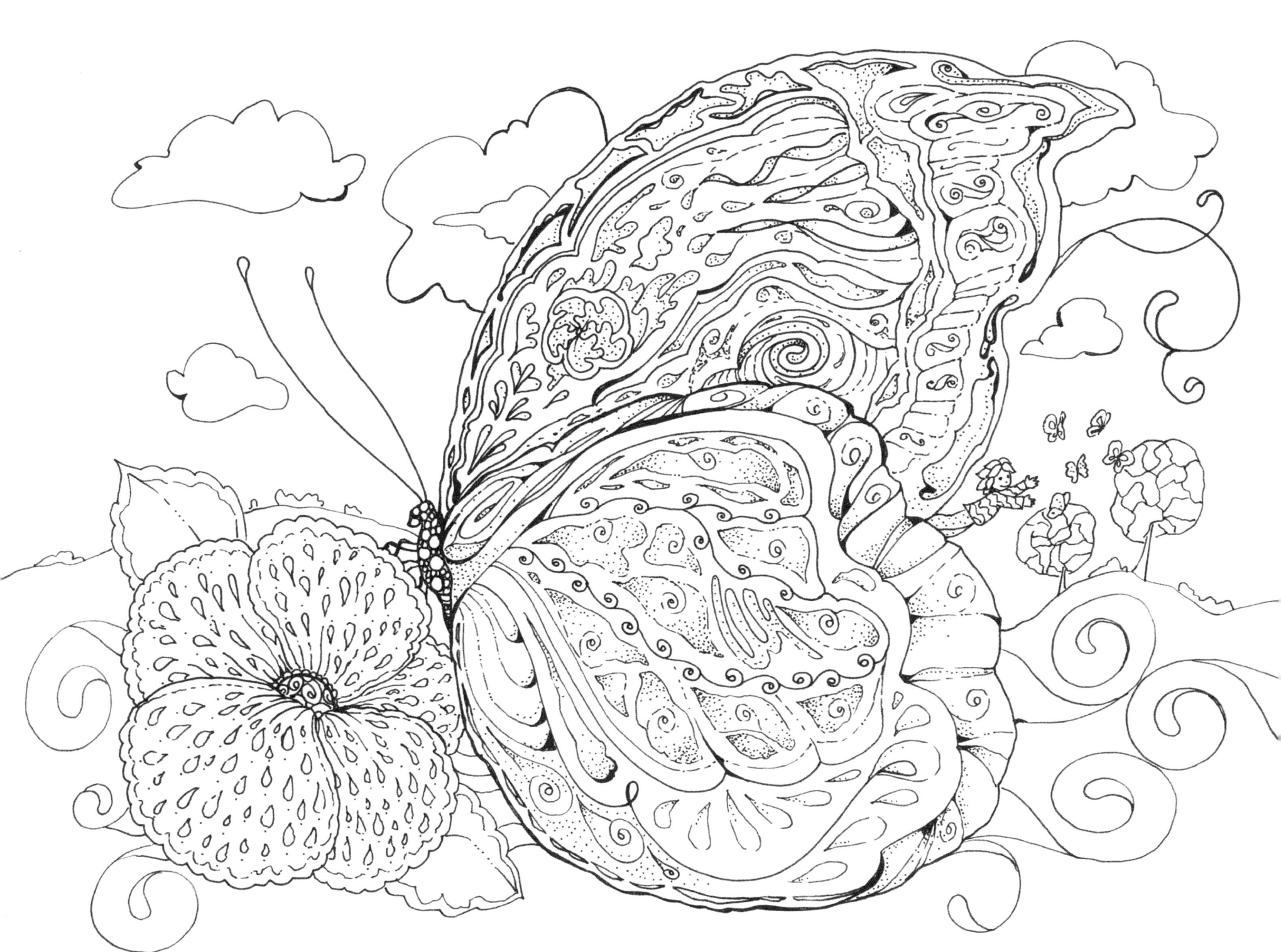

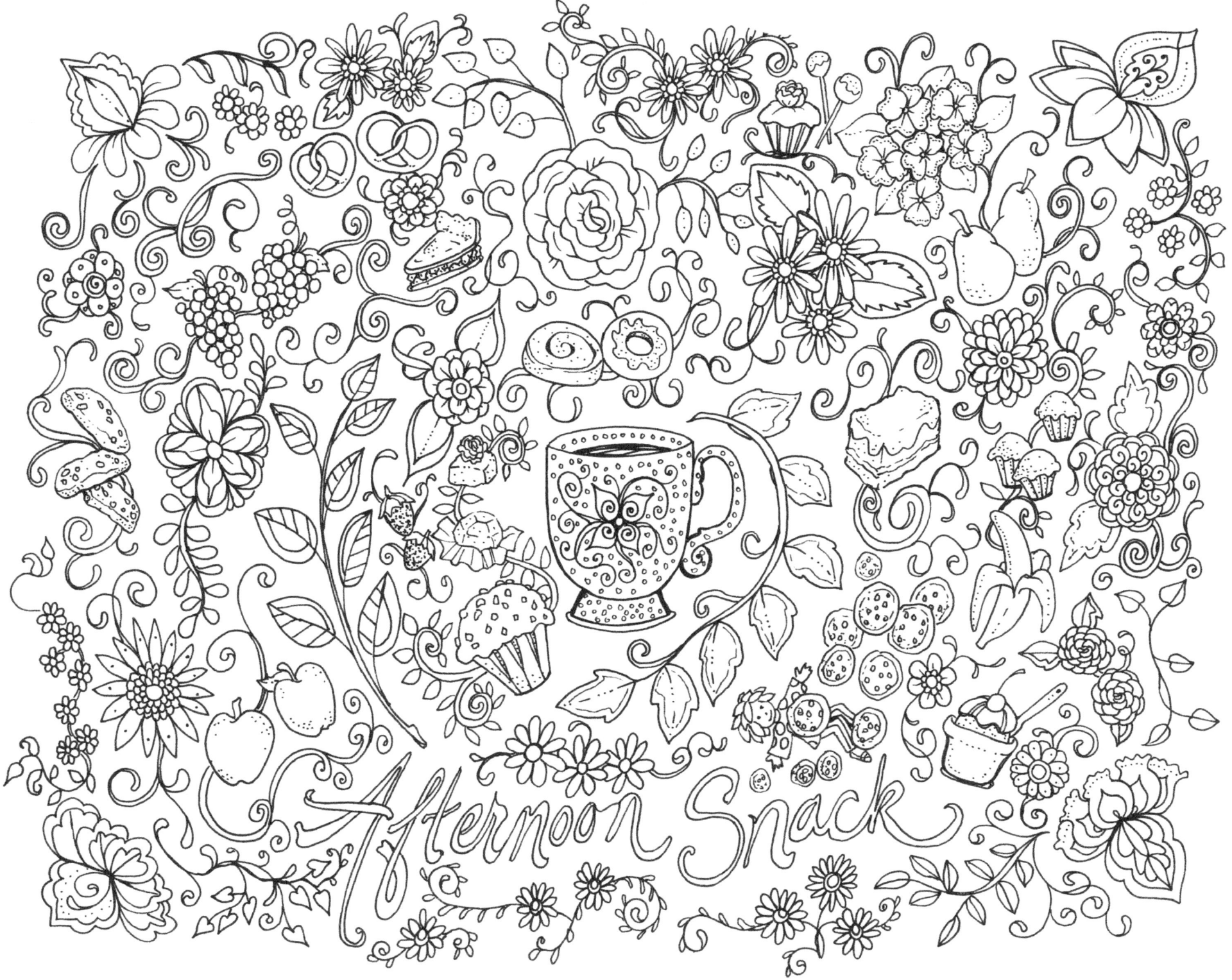

Afternoon Snack

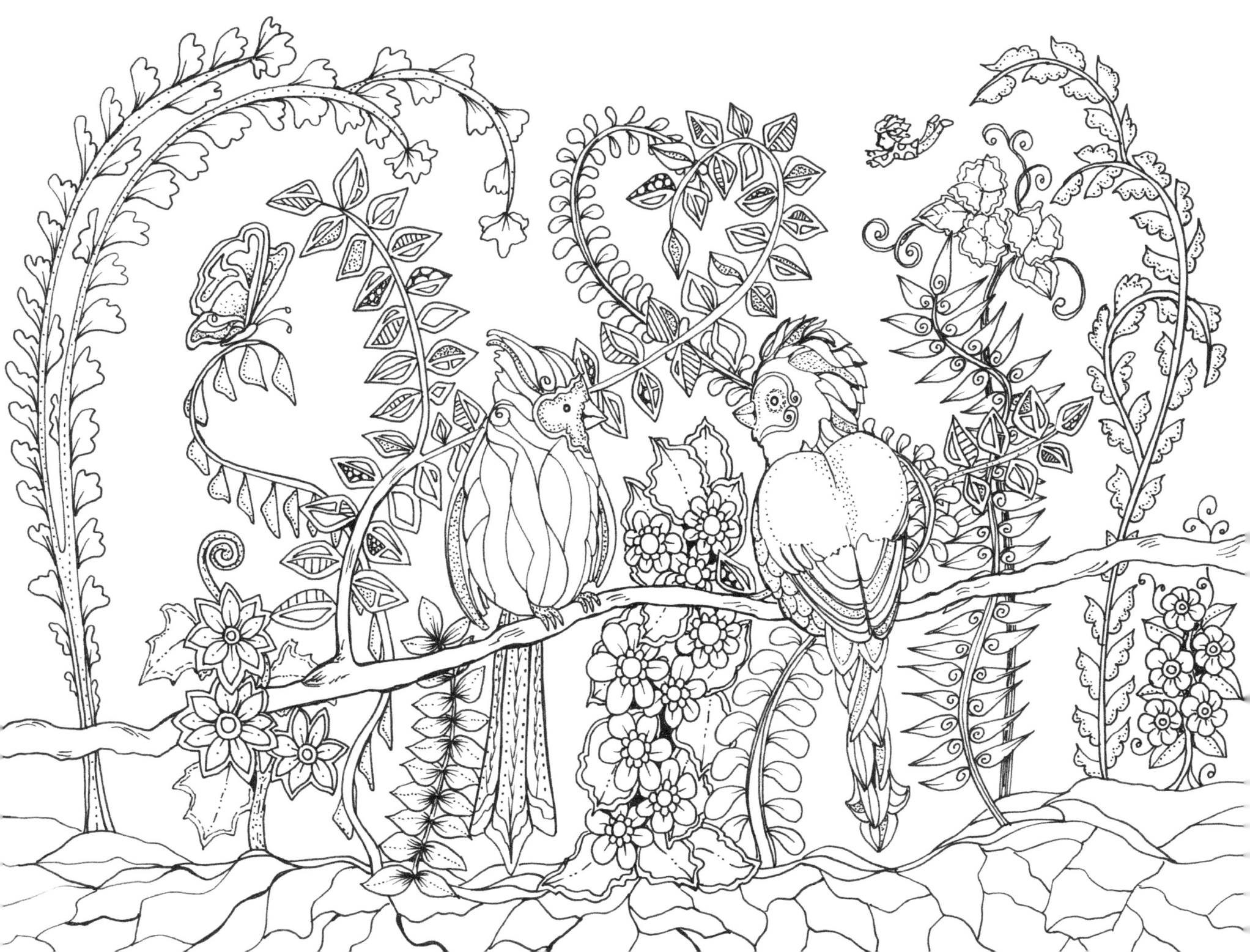

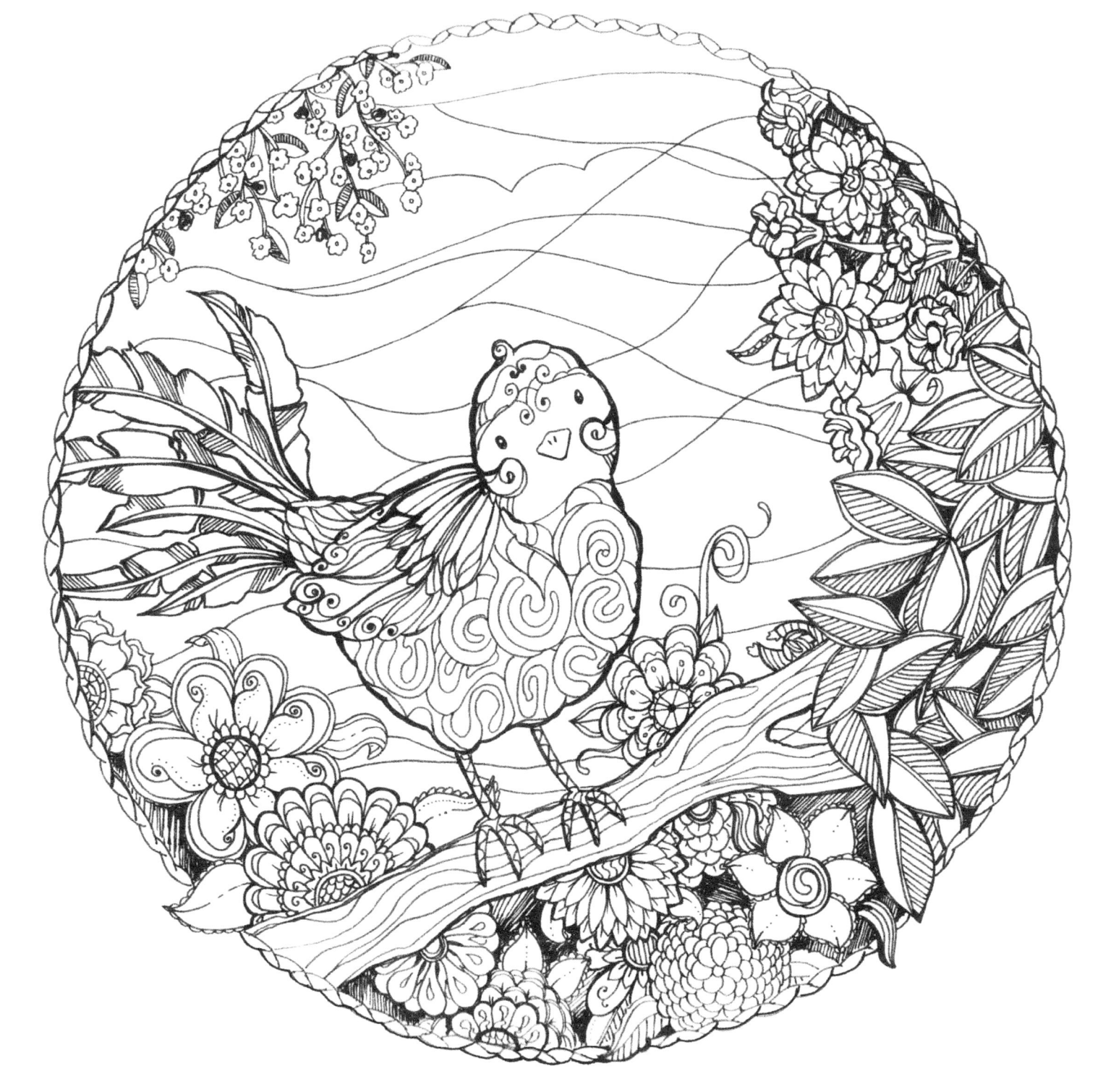

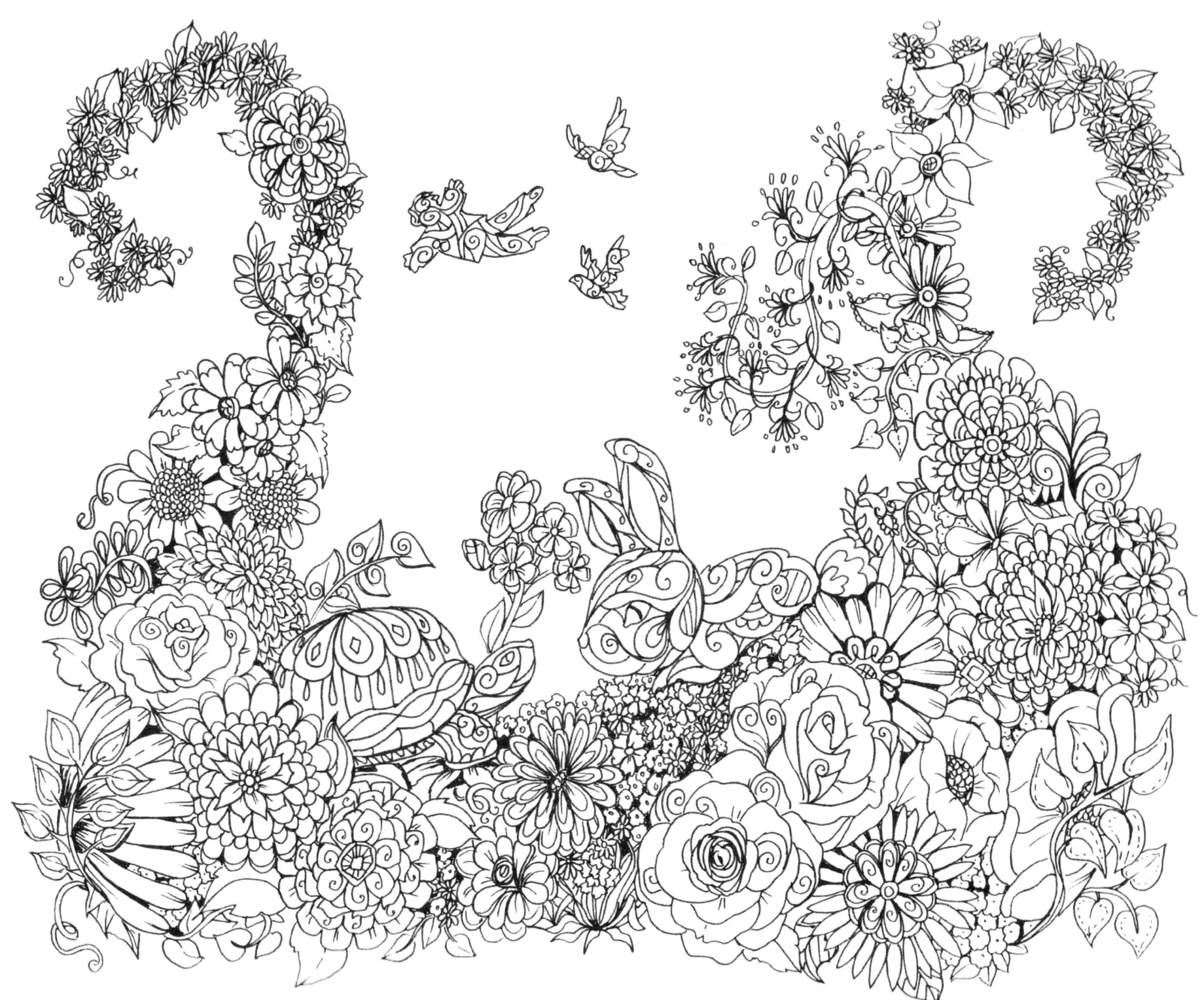

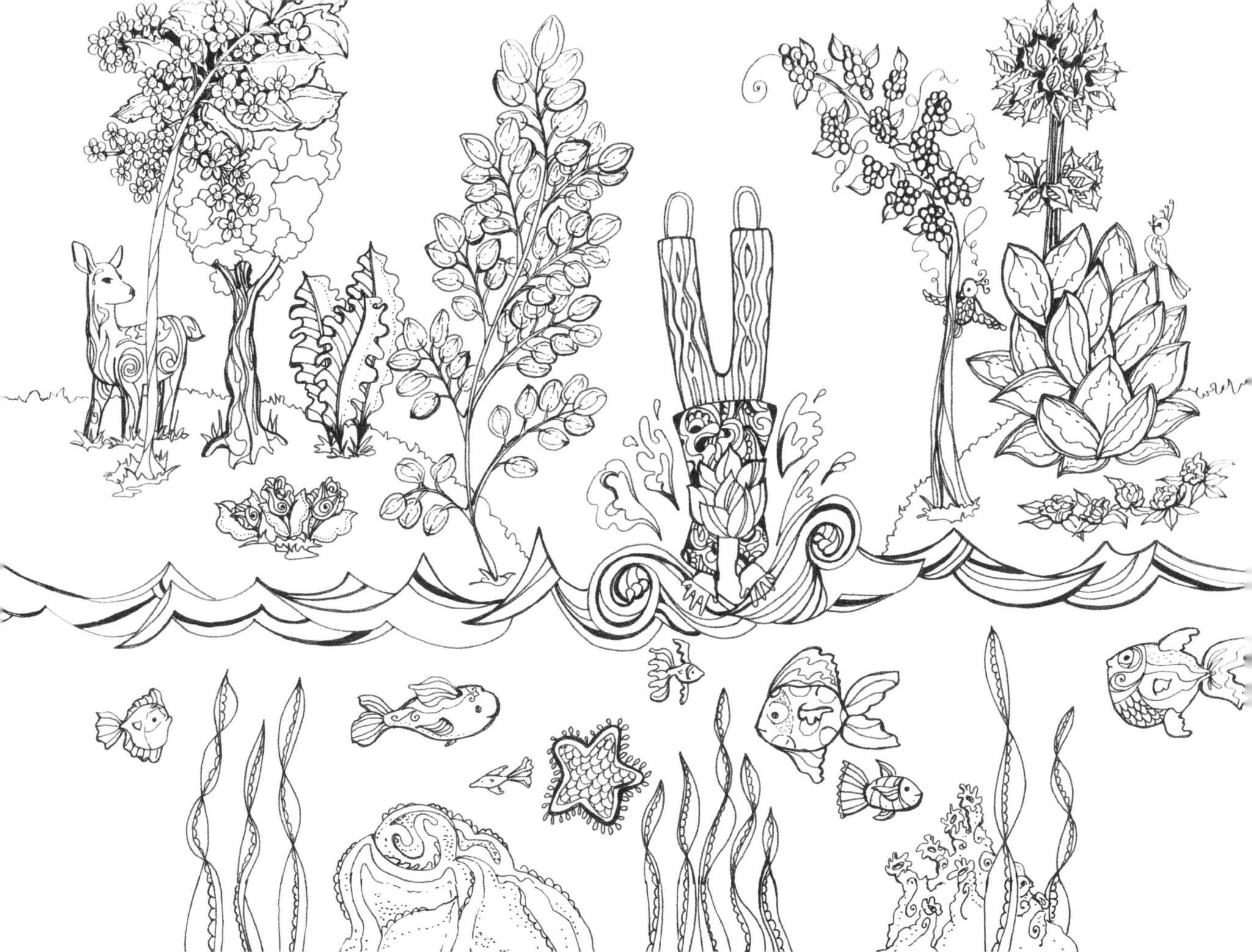

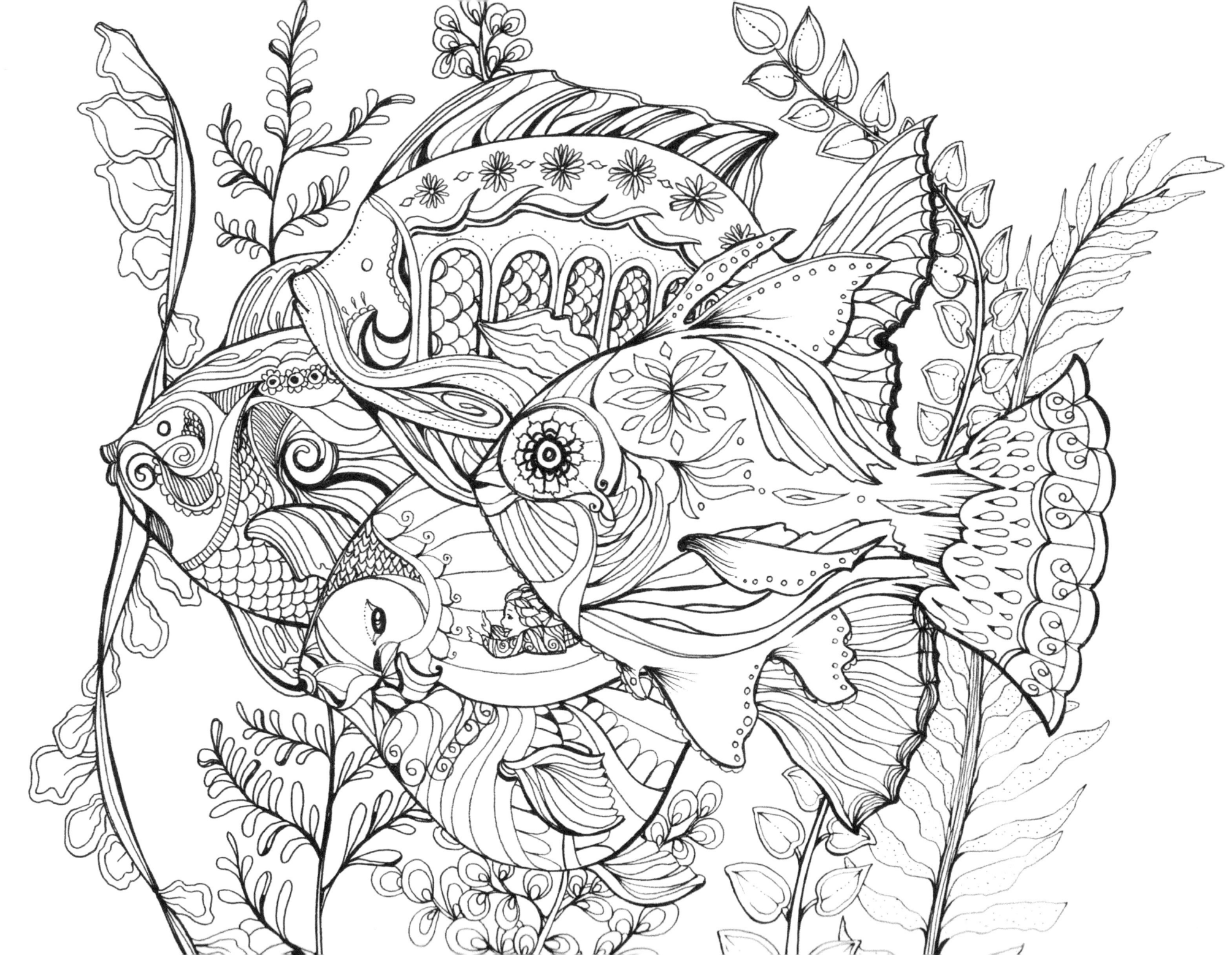

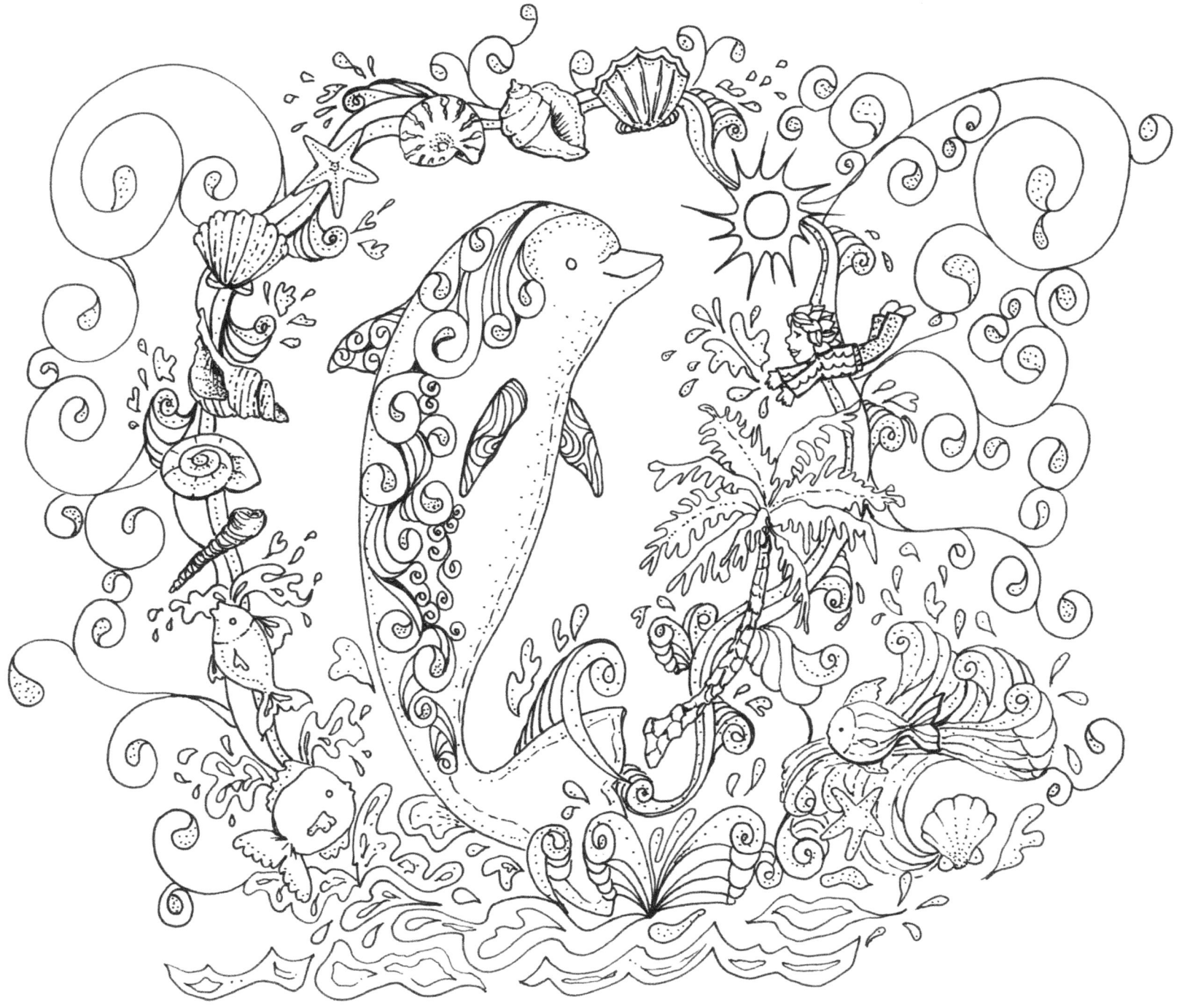

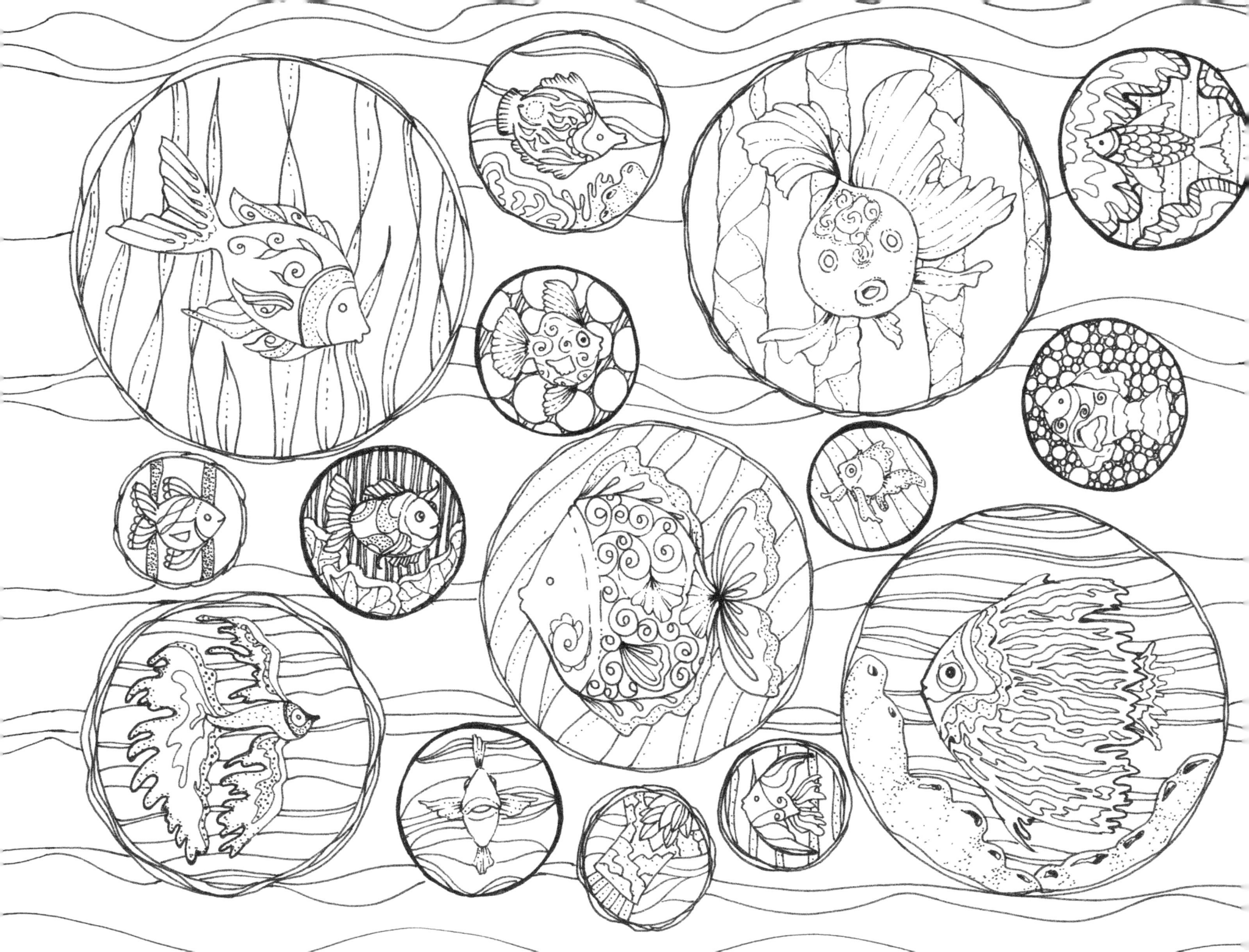

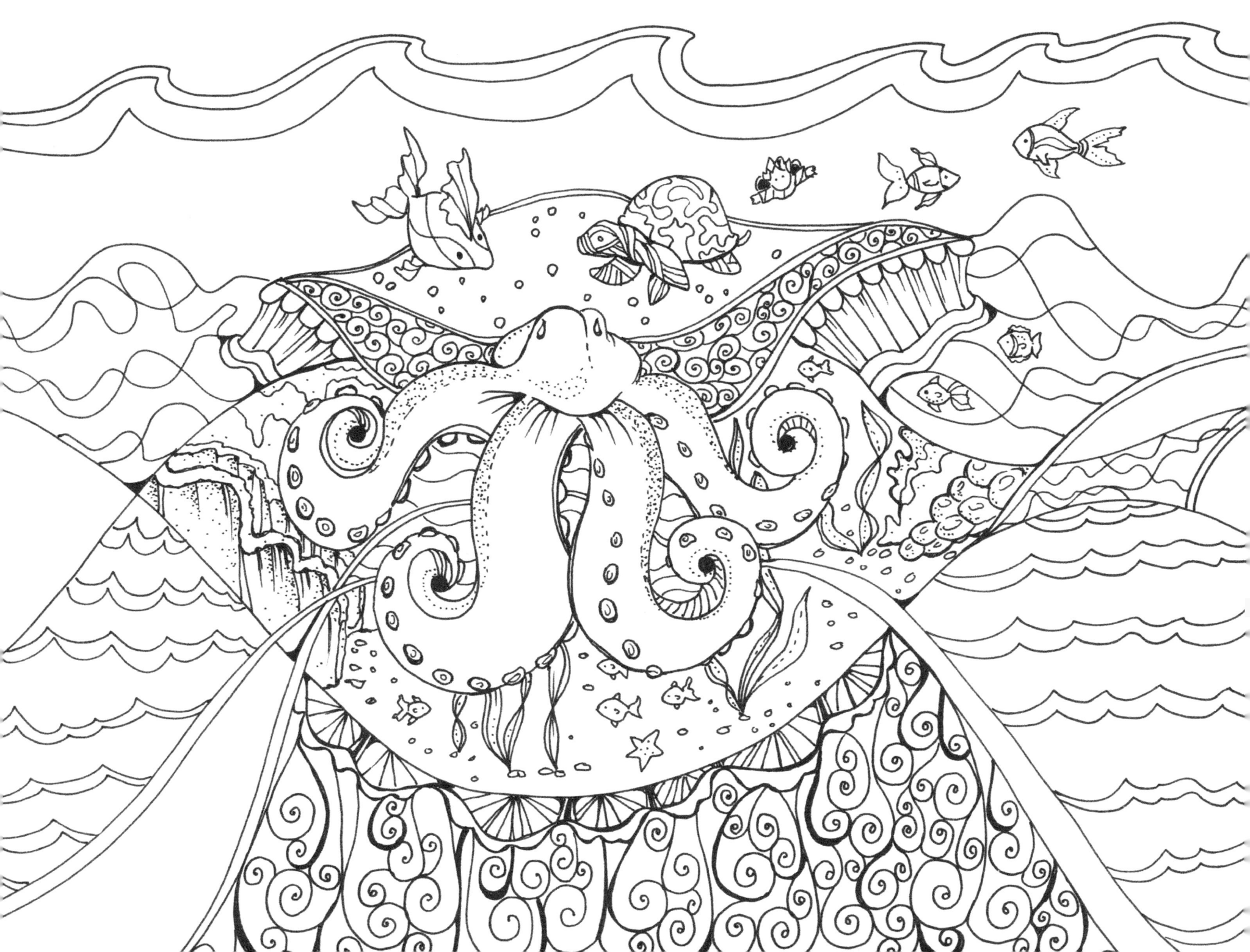

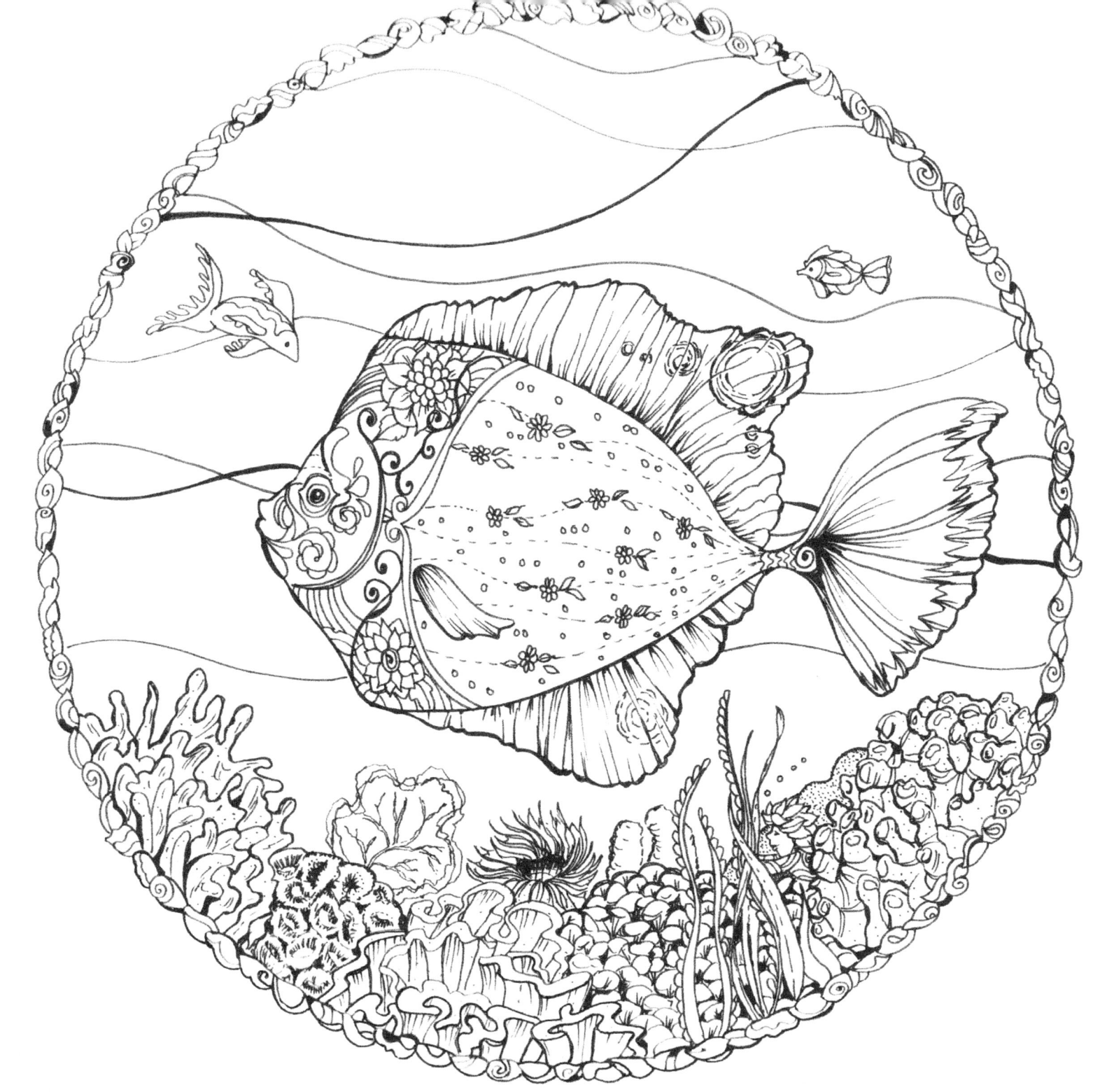

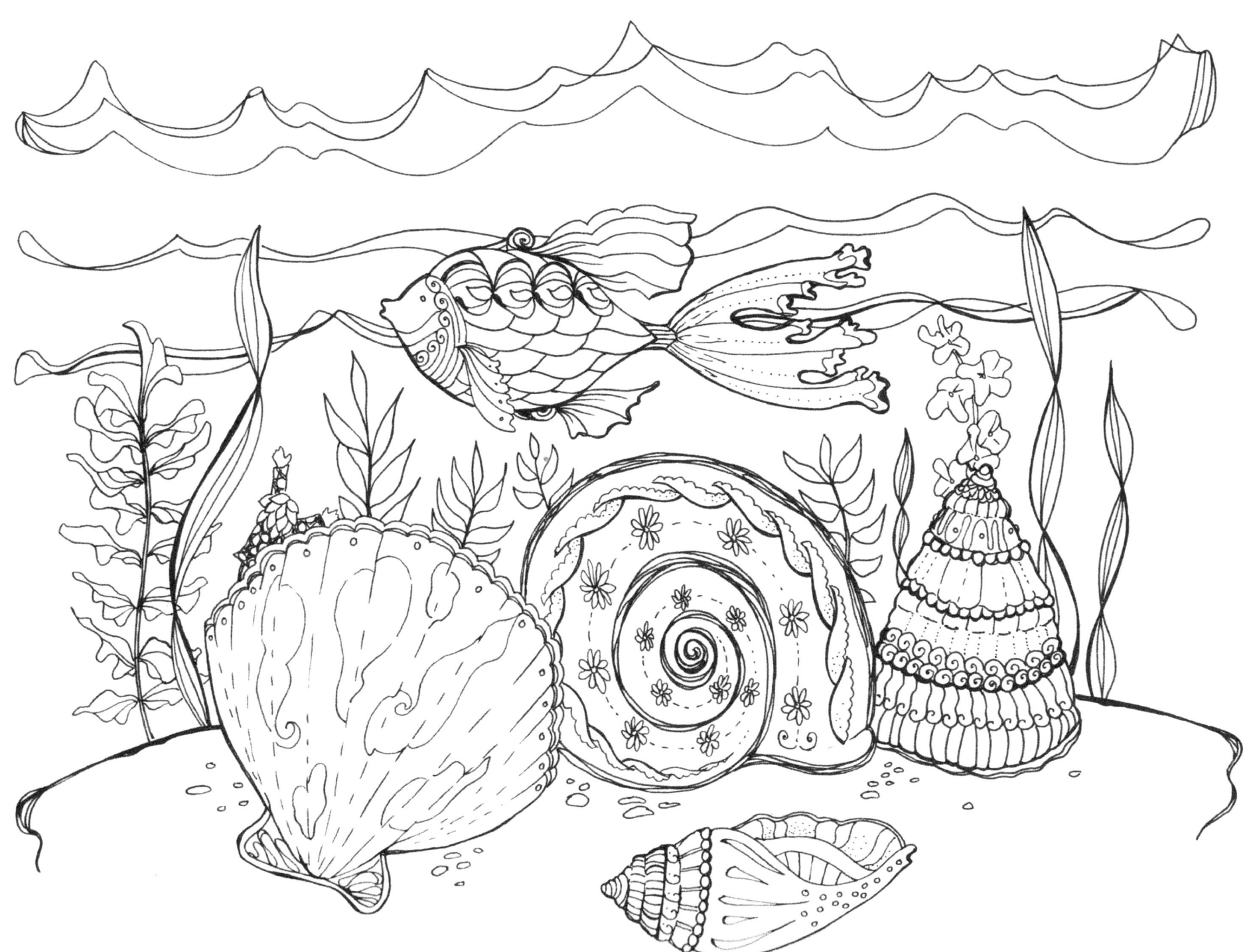

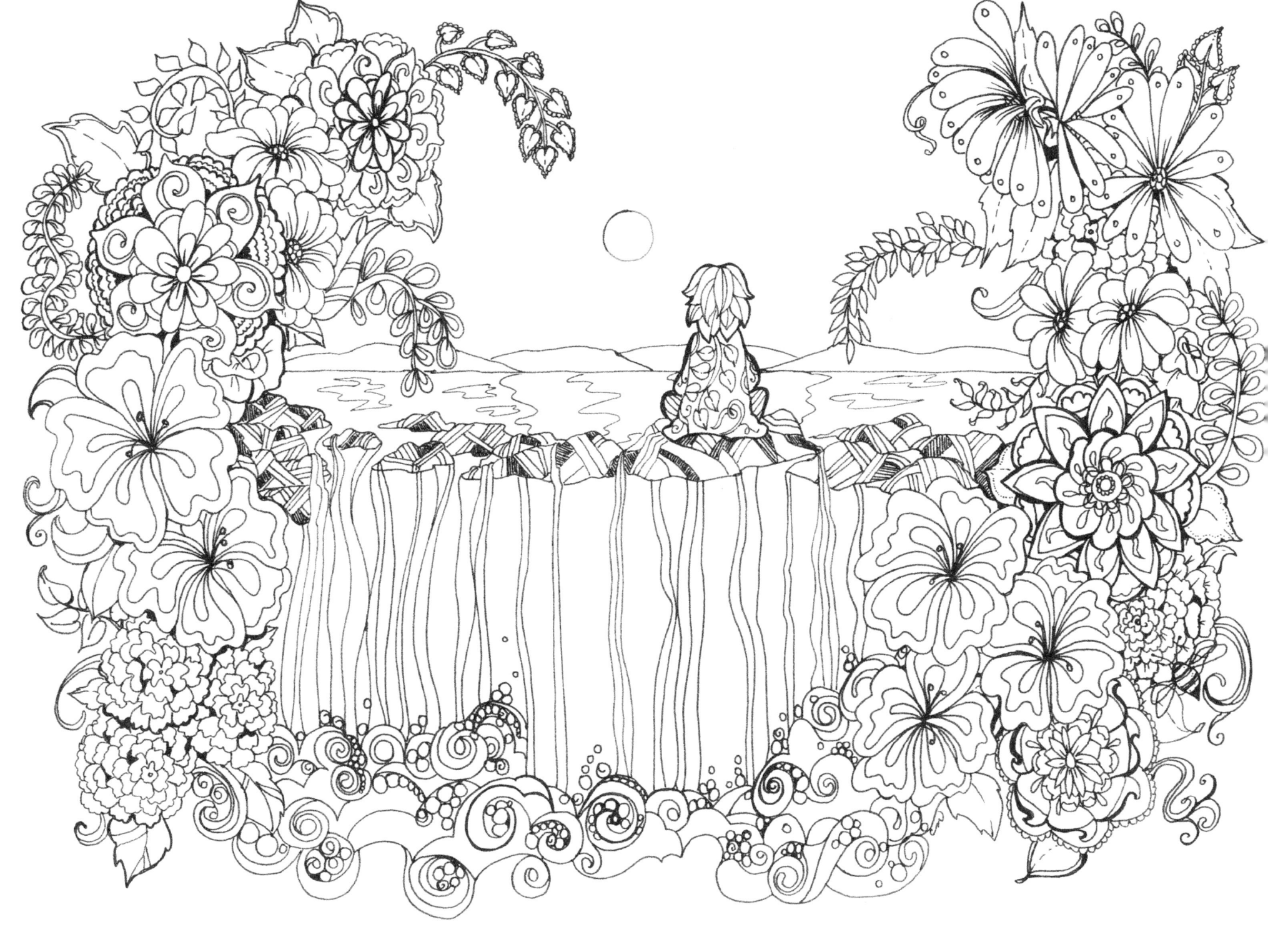

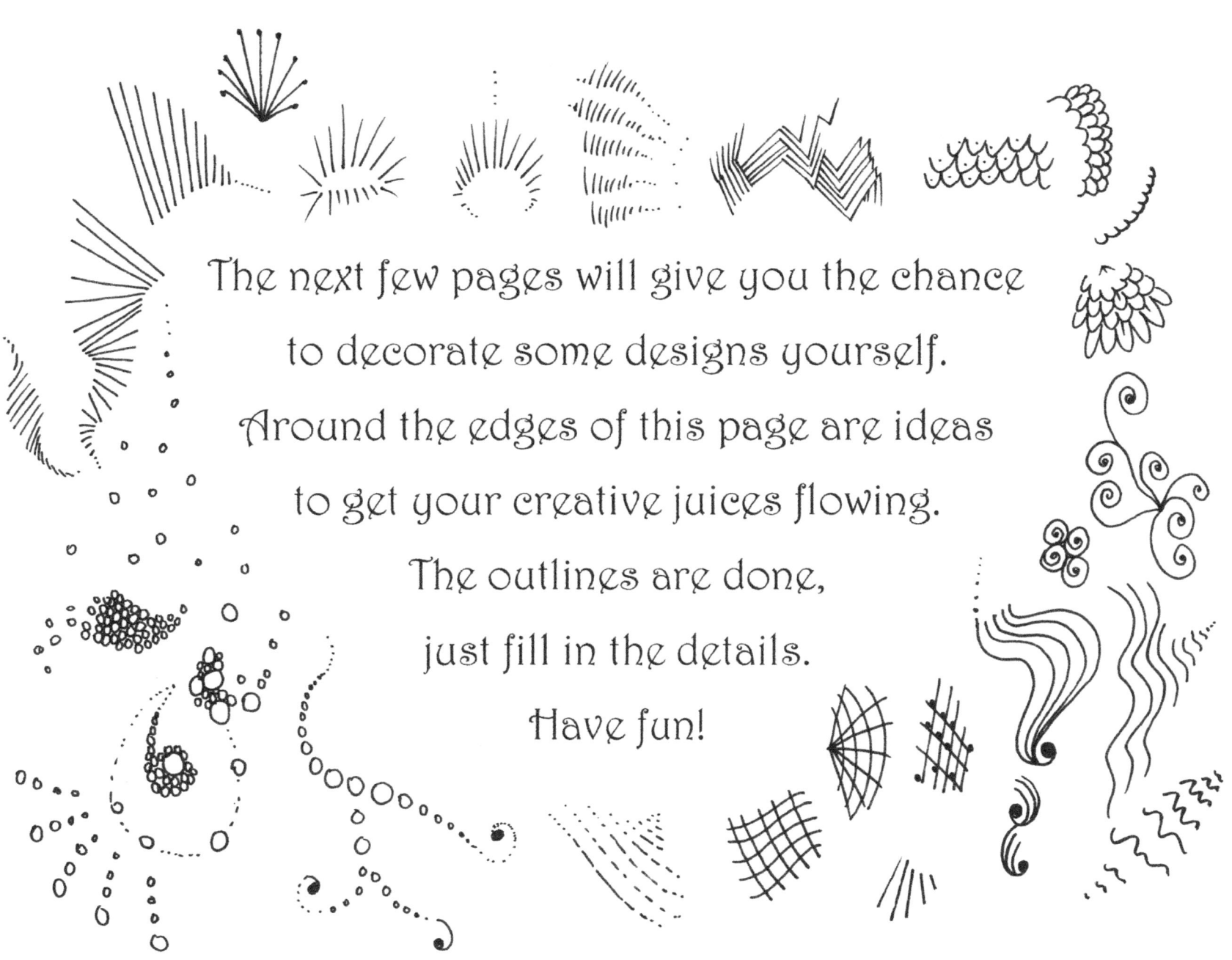

The next few pages will give you the chance
to decorate some designs yourself.
Around the edges of this page are ideas
to get your creative juices flowing.
The outlines are done,
just fill in the details.
Have fun!

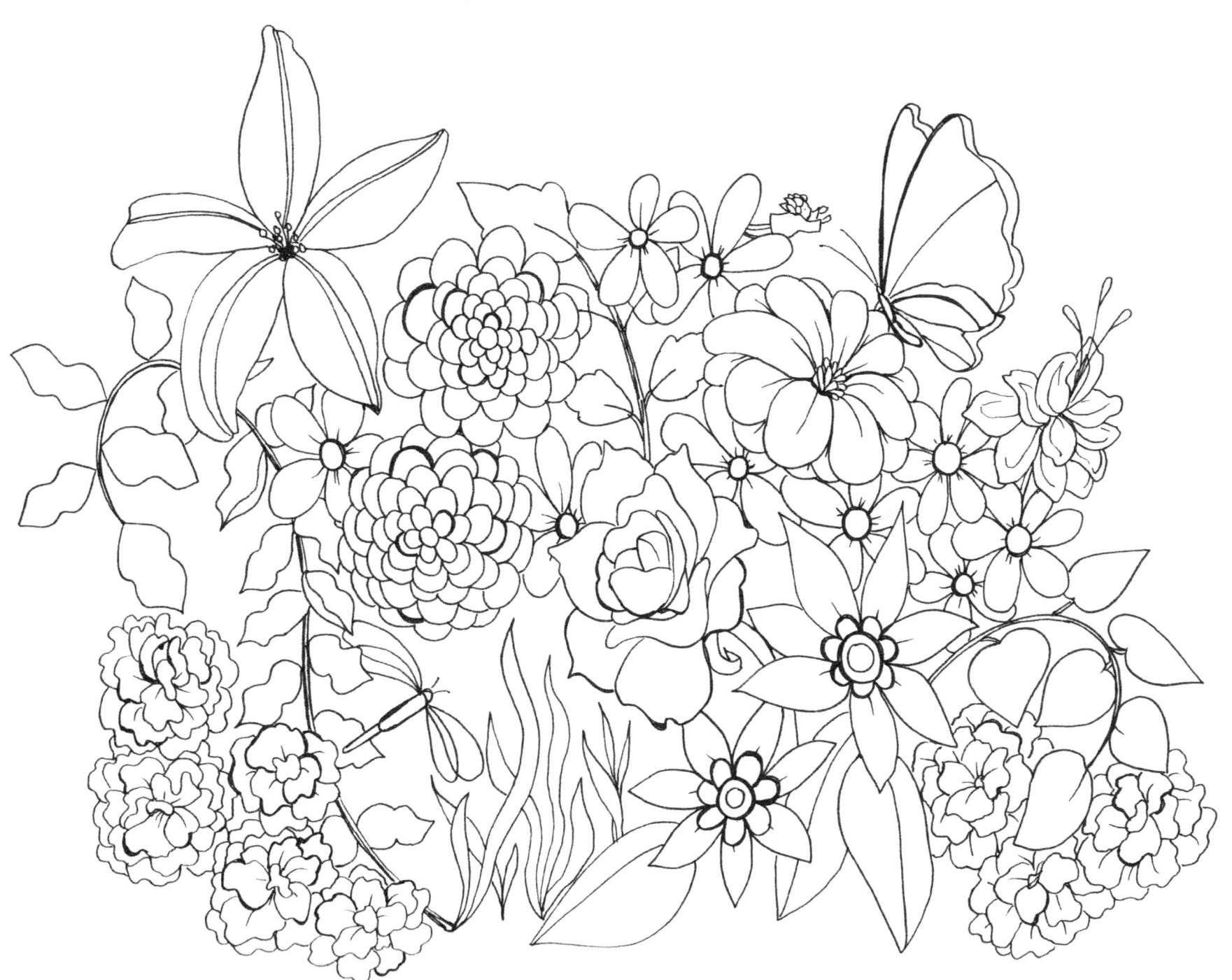

SUPPER

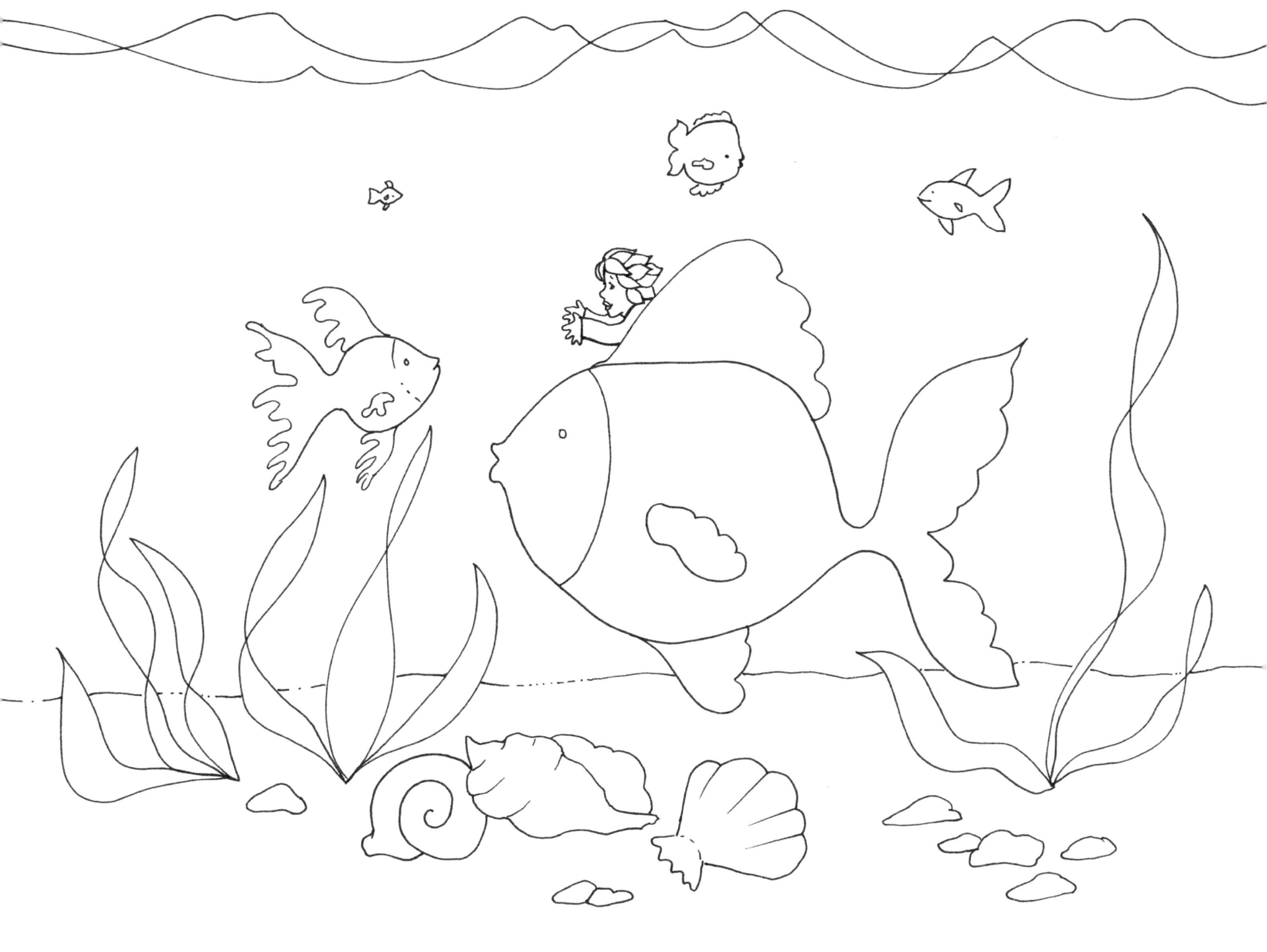

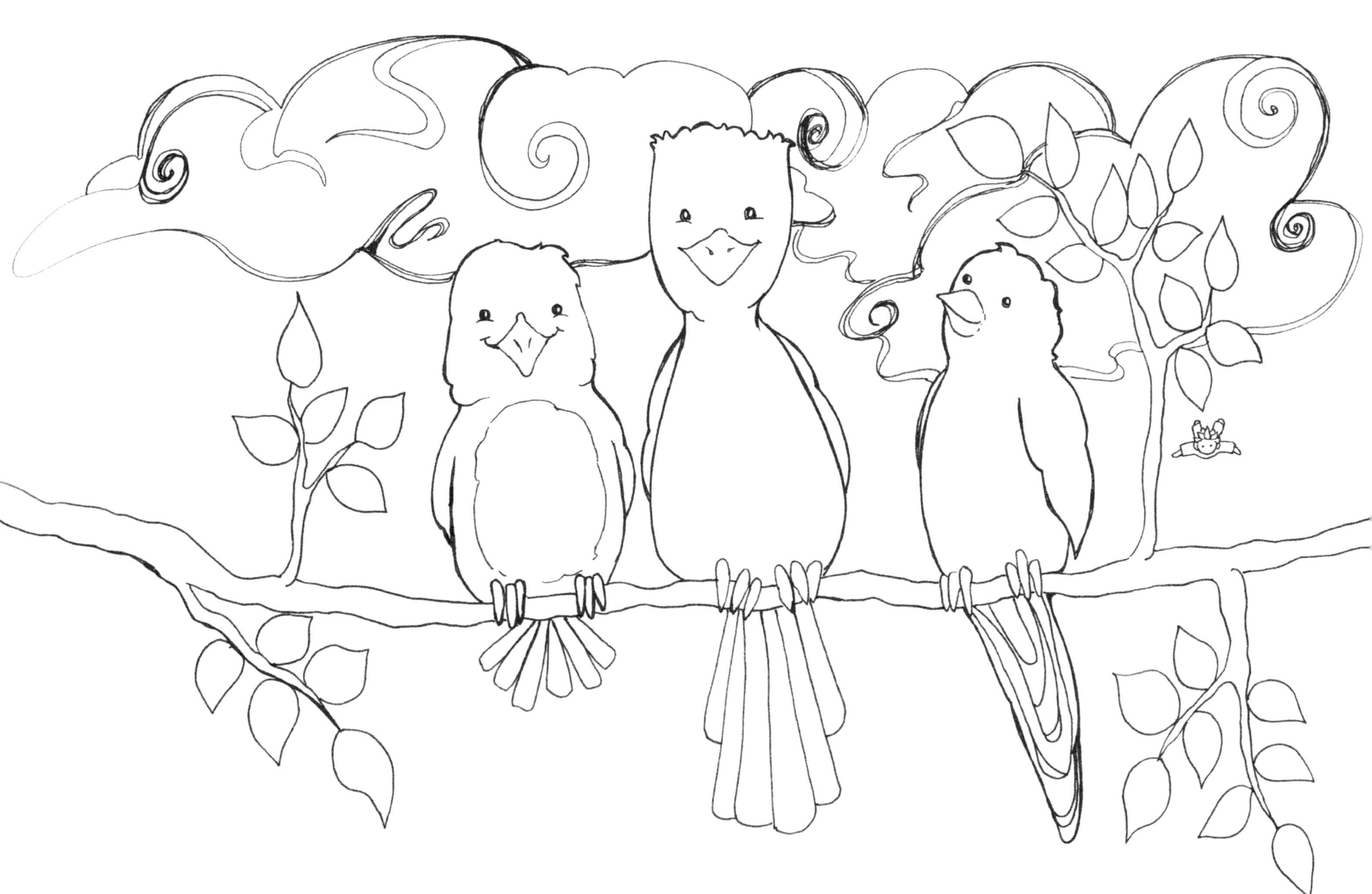

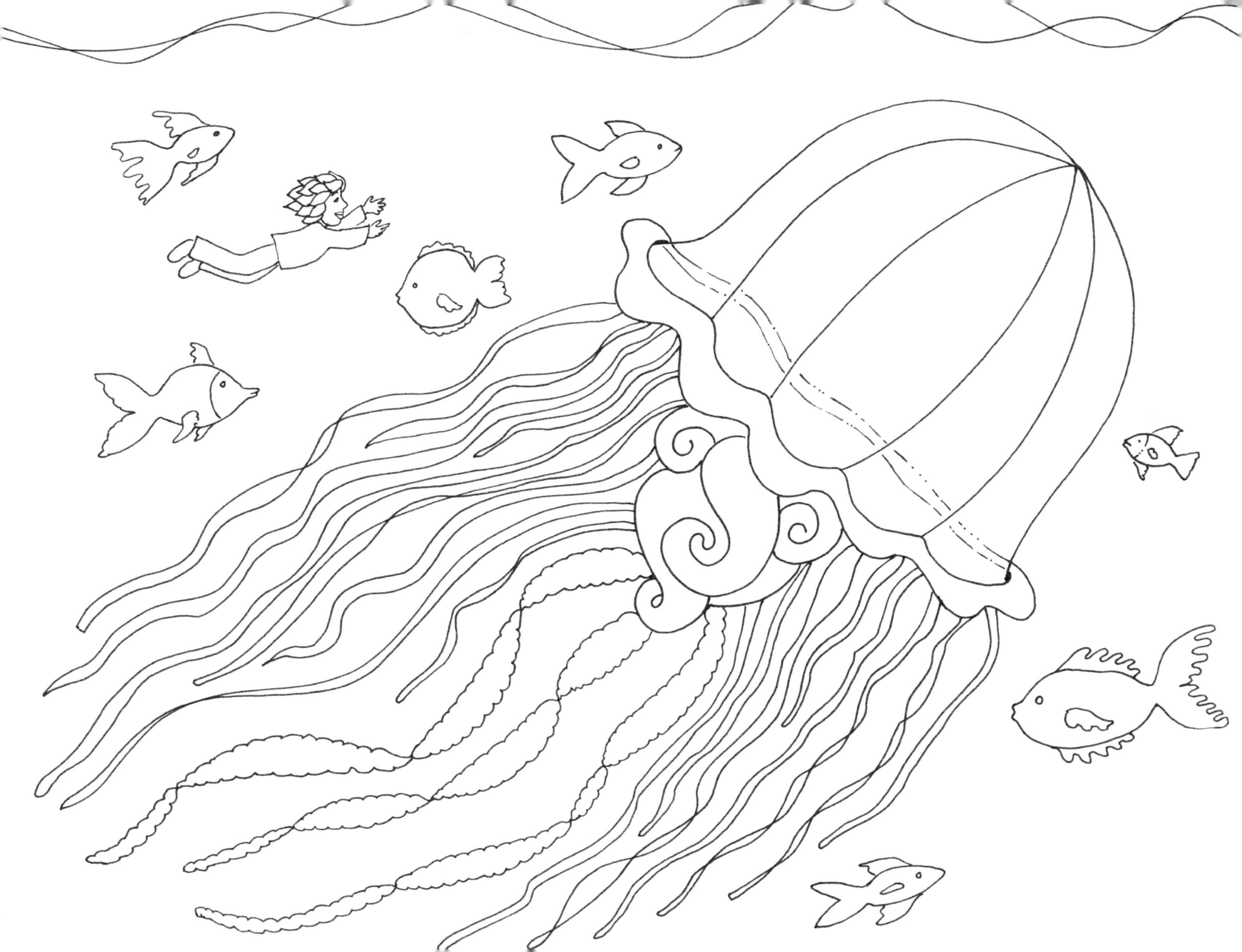

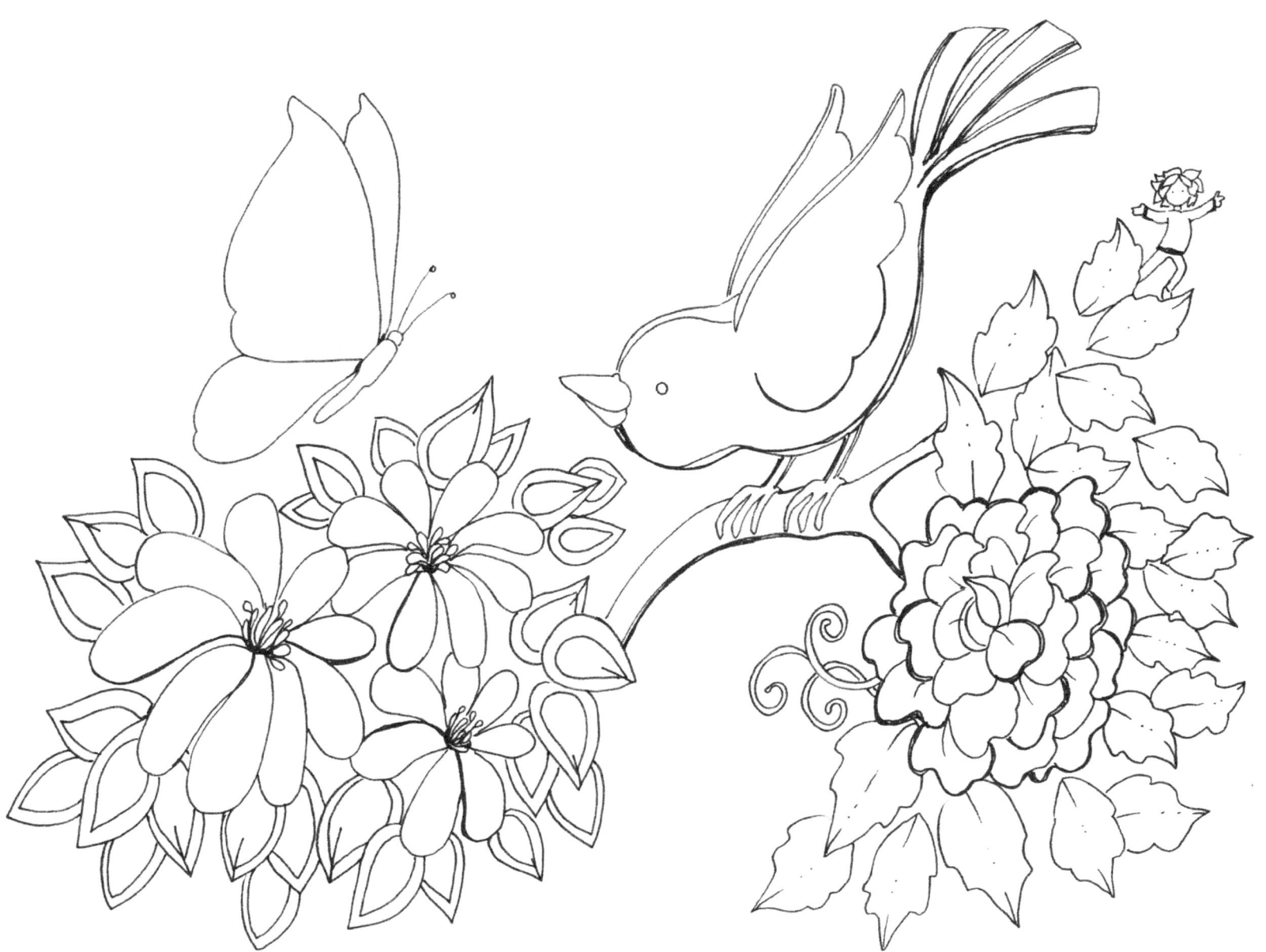

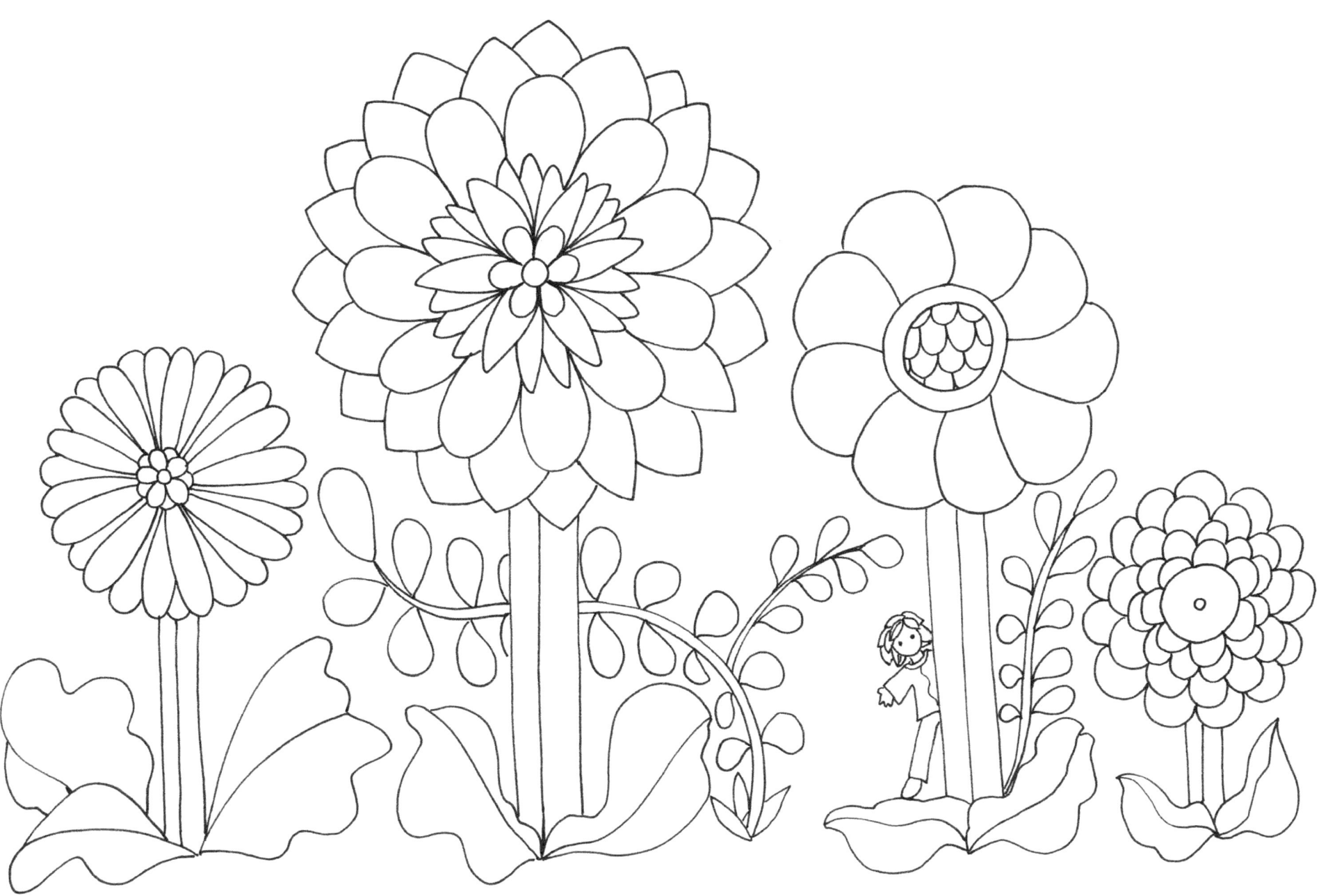

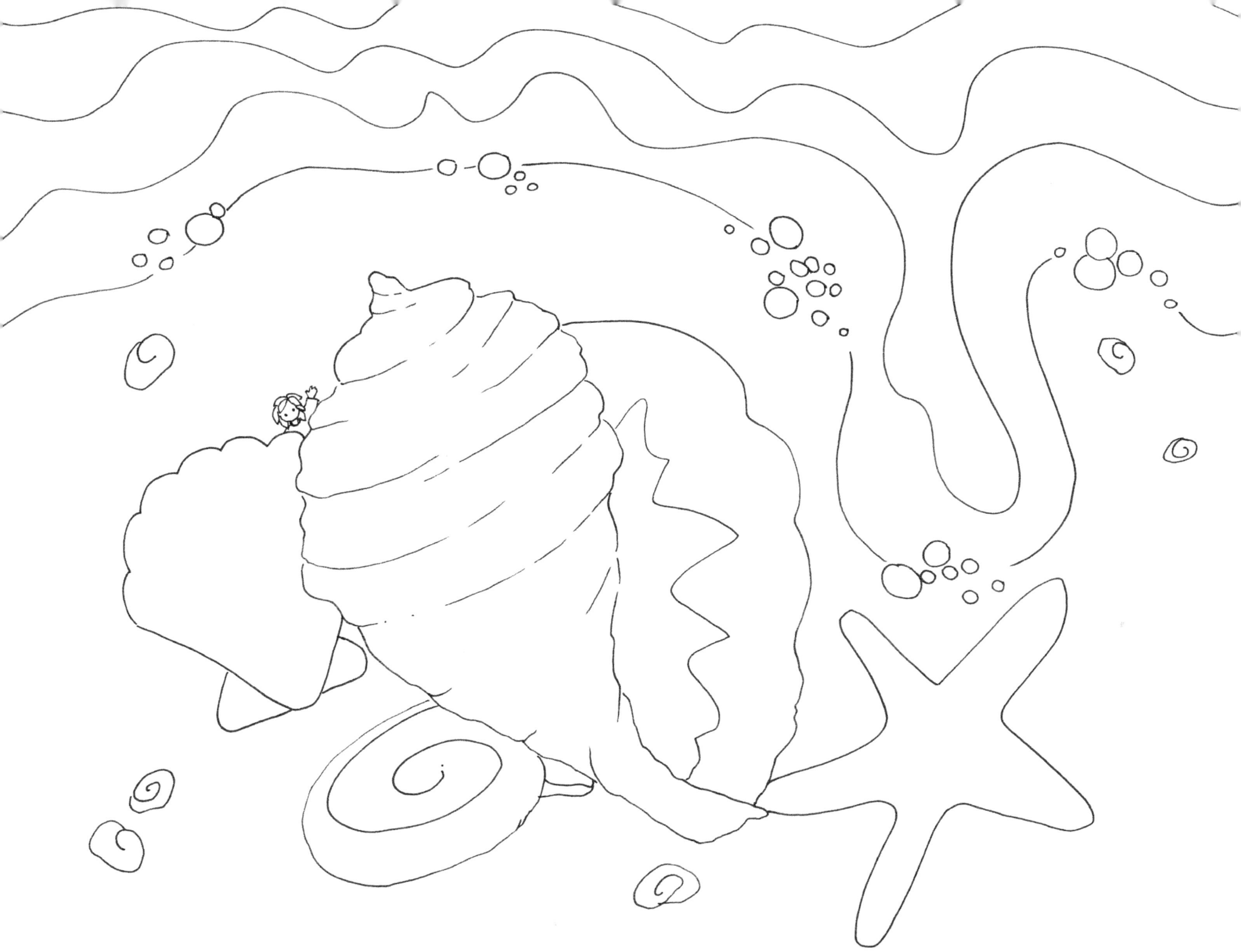

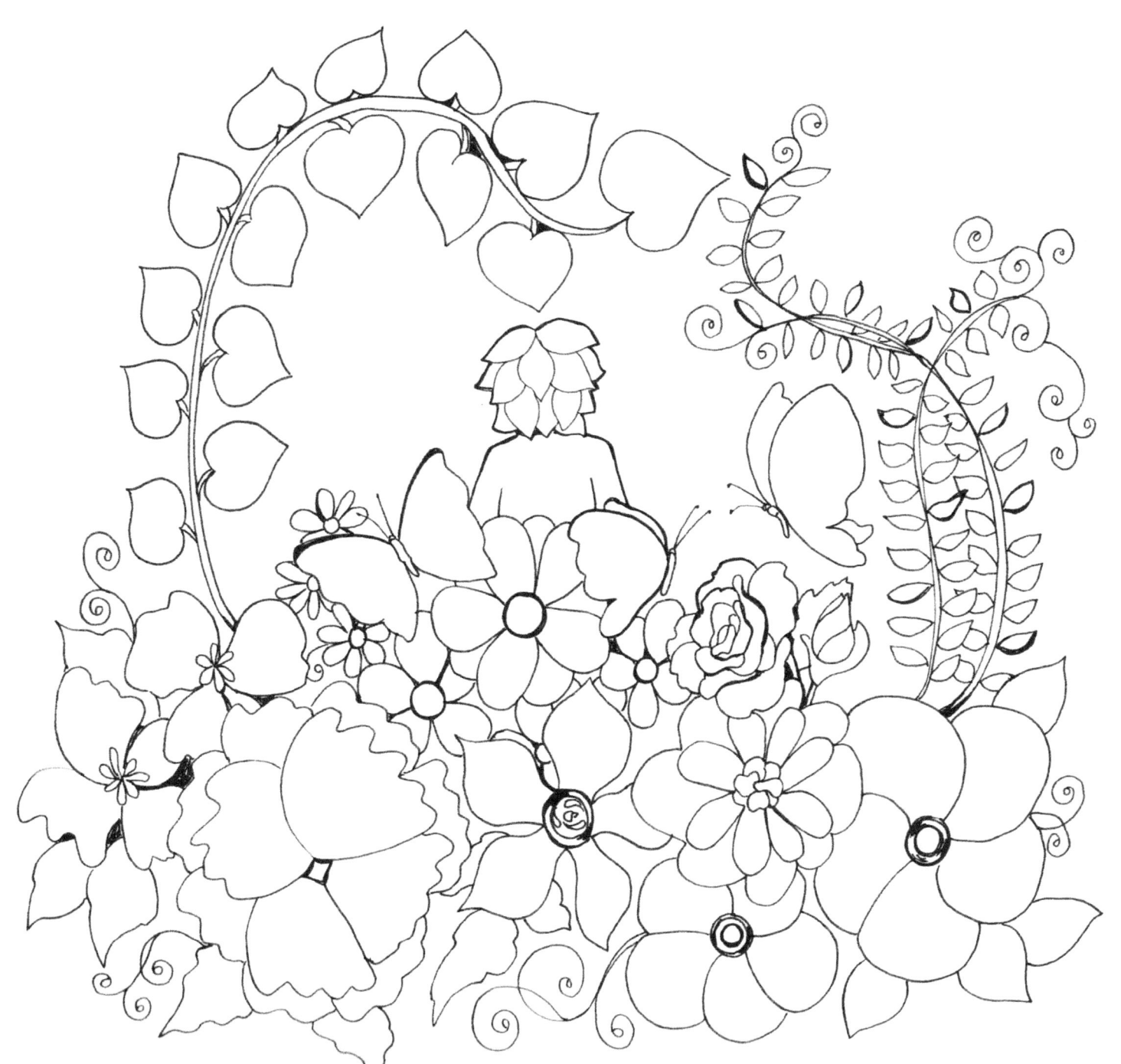

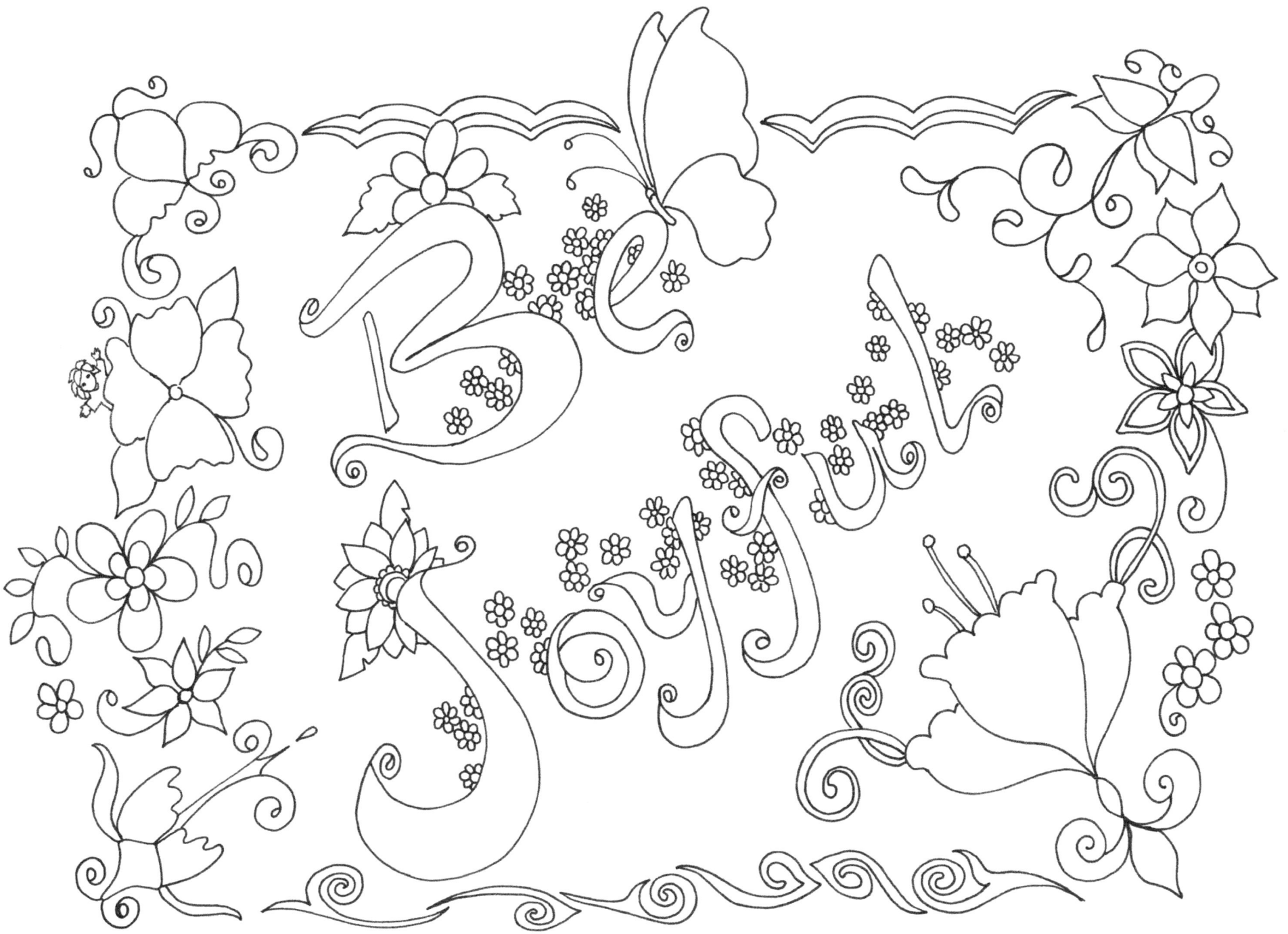